The Ego and Its Hyperstate

A Psychoanalytically Informed Dialectical Analysis of Self-Interest

The Ego and Its Hyperstate

A Psychoanalytically Informed Dialectical Analysis of Self-Interest

Eliot Rosenstock

Winchester, UK
Washington, USA

JOHN HUNT PUBLISHING

First published by Zero Books, 2021
Zero Books is an imprint of John Hunt Publishing Ltd., No. 3 East St., Alresford,
Hampshire SO24 9EE, UK
office@jhpbooks.com
www.johnhuntpublishing.com
www.zero-books.net

For distributor details and how to order please visit the 'Ordering' section on our website.

Text copyright: Eliot Rosenstock 2020

ISBN: 978 1 78904 513 0
978 1 78904 514 7 (ebook)
Library of Congress Control Number: 2020950333

A CIP catalogue record for this book is available from the British Library.

Design: Matthew Greenfield

UK: Printed and bound by CPI Group (UK) Ltd, Croydon, CR0 4YY
Printed in North America by CPI GPS partners

We operate a distinctive and ethical publishing philosophy in
all areas of our business, from our global network of authors to
production and worldwide distribution.

Contents

Also by the author

Žižek in the Clinic, Zero Books, ISBN: 978-1-78535-925-5

Introduction

Some Casual Remarks About This Text Existing Rather Than Not Existing

Self-interest is foundational to understanding the answer to the question of why something which is created by human beings exists. In this spirit, through these pages, for a few interested followers of that very question of "why," I will elucidate this seemingly simple notion known as "self-interest," and in doing so, unlock the forces of psychoanalysis and dialectical reasoning at this question of why self-interest can elucidate itself from a non-cohesive image into an incredible tool for understanding the very nature of reality qua the question of "why does this exist," as well as "what the hell is this," and not to forget, "oh God, what am I doing here, how did I get here, oh God, what do I do now?"

The self-interest camp in my personal circles is very split. Those who love to hear people talk about things in terms of self-interest need no convincing at the further elucidation of this idea which runs throughout reality. There are others, however, who seem to really like to hear me talk about other subjects within philosophy and psychology, and appear to glaze over when I bring up the idea of self-interest. These people ask me questions about their lives and the foundation of reality and what to do next, but when I hit the essence of the answer to that question, which is to say the notion of self-interest, it is like a great shot of anti-reality ideology pulses through them. As the robots in "Westworld" say when they see their own programming and the safeguard installed in them by their creators is activated, "it doesn't look like anything to me." The anti-psychotic jolt of the other is visible to me clearly when discussing self-interest to a party who doesn't really accept its foundational quality to

1

existence, wants people to think of things in terms of idea qua the idea, or qua a neurotic fantasy, not qua self-interest. Self-interest is a dirty concept, like sex, but unlike sex, it suggests singularity which threatens the multiplicity of the universe. If one understood the concept of self-interest as a process thoroughly, however, the dreamlike nature of reality would reveal itself, and what appeared initially as an anti-psychotic singularizing would reveal itself to be a highly rational map of human events through the passage of time.

Theories, or more accurately stated, crude images and rhetorical devices involving self-interest, have mainly concerned themselves with power and with fantasies which mimic the libidinal death-drives of kings, capitalists, and criminals. This misses a key component to self-interest, however, which is the perception and engagement with the fabric of reality itself. Along with the introduction of psychoanalytic concepts of the unconscious, we can get a picture of rational self-interest which works to identify the process of self-interest and how one can rationally engage with it and in its course, engage with reality itself in a manner conducive to that process.

The misunderstanding of self-interest is due to viewing it as a single point in time rather than the dynamic creation and destruction of what is really existing in the world. In this sense, it is a very useful thing to know the process of self-interest which I will outline briefly here. The power hungry who identify with an image of self-interest enemies and benefit from the misconstruing of self-interest, both the exploiter and the childish hedonist, know what they are doing is correct thanks to self-interest, and the moral man of society knows the childish hedonist is bad because he, yes, acts only on his self-interest.

One problem, this is not actually the substantive process of self-interest. I will show you how self-interest aligns with the discoveries of psychoanalysis, against the double obfuscation of those who take up the banner of self-interest in the name of simple immediate demand contra society at large, as well as against those who with Christ-like devotion, sing the song of reality contra self-interest, positing a moral function as being-for-other. This is equally absurd and immediately disavows the psychological nature of reality.

The world is filled with the synthetic waking-dream material of everyone. These dreams have material backing, and to state the obvious, these dreams are not dreams at all, but the actual content of the world when we open our eyes and call ourselves awake. This has consequences in all realms of reality which have interest to us, and our self-interest distorts all logics and bends all logics toward it. Self-interest is a theory of gravity in this sense.

There is a process or a metalogic to reality which hides behind the veil of our immediate perception. When language becomes involved, logic becomes something which takes place outside of the realm of a single consciousness, it becomes a sort of consensus, a group rationality. But the rationality is always struck through by their dreamlike origins, and insofar as they contradict those dreamlike origins, we are affected thoroughly by discontents of external logic, and it always bends with the gravity of self-interest.

It is not difficult to disrupt the imaginary category of self-interest which is seen as something which is against the interest of others. This is a zero-sum fallacy, in that the content of the world as created through the dream logic has the same gravity in which the dreamer creates his or her world while asleep. Self-interest is not a simple vulgar childish "mine," but the nature of reality itself. The problem is that it is easily repressed, this nature of reality being related to self-interest, and people immediately move past this aspect of reality to assess the world with various rhetorics which would like to forget that there is a fantasy underlying their world, which is to say there is a gap.

As we define self-interest, we will discover reality itself

begins to open up to us. This reality has a rationality. The mining of the rationality of the irrational will reveal to us the rationality of being, which is irrational and rational. It is material, as well as fantastical. Material is created solely because of its fantastical qualities, which is to say their Freudian properties, and thus to understand reality, we must understand the fantasy. Fantasy is clearly not simply an unreality, but a key component of reality itself. When this is ignored, structures begin to become symptomatic as it is not known that structures are in fact vessels for this strange essence which is the process of self-interest.

No matter where we go, the psychoanalyst comes up against the question of what makes self-interest, but it is rarely if ever addressed as such. Psychoanalysis is not necessarily for the bolstering of a person, for their stated interests, but something which undermines. Nonetheless, meet an analyst and you will see that he is surely bolstered by this undermining, made into something more definite, if not always something beautiful.

This undermining and challenging leads the subject of analysis in the process, and when one moves toward the process rather than the simple imaginary notion, self-interest appears, which is to say reality itself emerges somewhat from behind its veil of obfuscation, and the self-interest machine of the analysand can make appropriate adjustments based on a more accurate map of reality, which is to say a map of one's own self and what concerns the self. What concerns the self? Anything the self wants to be concerned with, and thus the map of reality is not just for the self, but extends beyond the self into knowing the world, and the self as component as well as conscious perceiver of the world.

We rest a little easier in the knowledge that our gaze does not have to turn maddeningly deep into the molecules themselves, but that signifiers themselves become molecules and have their own logic. The ego has various things which it concerns itself with, and becomes various processes. This jumping and movement, as well as its overlapping and becoming these processes, is The Ego's Hyperstate. It's not that the ego has its hyperstate, but the ego is its hyperstate. The ego may be an image, but it's also a process. **We will be investigating the ego not as image, but in its movements and forms of other things which become the concrete material of self-interest and which is a process we can know as its "hyperstate." We can know these hyperstates as the real movement of ideals in the world, producing meaning as they produce symptoms. The movement of history producing a cascading effect of material appearance and disappearance, ideal jockeying, which is the Actual content of self-interest.**

Throughout this book, we will extend every ideal into something like a string or register. The language of the ideal is not simply a computer program, but it ties together in a weave to give us the appearance of the a priori synthetic reality. This weave becomes articulated in various manners, and movement represents the ideal within the world, the actuality of self-interest. The rationality of the ideal gives us access to the multiplicity of functions which the ego performs, and moves them from their unconscious molecular form, from displacement, into the realm of rationality. The register is not just in the psyche, but tied to the material of the world with itself. It is with this in mind that we can begin to discuss self-interest, although this is imaginary as well as we, of course, have already begun.

The feelings which cut through the body as well as the cool logics placed meekly outside the body become self-interest as they interact and learn to articulate themselves in the form of the register which they originally were, as well as registers which neither were in the first place. As we become accustomed to something, we sometimes forget what we had in mind, we jump registers, or we add another string. Psychological processes are clearly at work in the differences in our opinions regarding various subjects, but this process is the process of the ego and its hyperstate.

When we look at the world in this manner we begin to understand the bizarre situations which pepper our psychic and material landscapes which seem to clash against each other, and we can see how the knotting and tangling of the series of ideas and determinate features of reality appear as rational which was seen previously as pure irrationality; through various registers these irrational aspects of existence reveal a rationality of the irrational, of fantasy completion, and extension.

To understand the task ahead, I will briefly become my own critic: If all language is woven, what in God's name is a "rational" self-interest? If self-interest is like gravity, then what good is there in having a self-interest which is rational? The knowledge of the process does not always pay fidelity to the force to the process which is the original nature of the gravitational pull of an act, and so what good is it to have rationality at all?

Simply put, rationality is what is required to gain access to the substance of reality. There is a singularity, but rather than a computer knowing itself, the human is knowing itself as self-interest. Once this happens, the material of being becomes workable in a way which it never was before.

Not all desire rationality, but there is a rationality possible which is tied to self-interest. The second movement of reflected self-interest, which is to say rational self-interest, opens up when considering reason as the multiplicity of uses of an incomplete idea which produces various registers and knots, fantasies producing fantasies, logics producing logics. This is not always done directly, but done from the side, through the introduction of new logics, of new registers, by people who may not even know the initial weave in the first place.

In the fantasy's quality as empty potentiality, an ideological surplus which may first deceive us into thinking them of complete things in and of themselves, something singular, can be seen as something else entirely, its nature which is within being of others, something which can be tampered with.

A quick communist fantasy: a Marxist grabs a hold of the means of production in order to stem the tide of bourgeoise idealism, which attempts to tie fantasy to itself without considering the fantasy's material nature. The fantasy in the world is material, and the force of money is obfuscated to the point where it seems that money is the primary driver of itself due to its ability to accumulate itself. For the Marxist, money accumulating money becomes territory for the ideal of Marxism. Within this territory, ideals of a fair workplace can be instituted. However, because a Marxist is a person and not simply a Marxist, how this occurs will be through the Marxist's idea of the "Good Cause" of Marxism. Thus, one might get a workplace that runs like any other workplace, or one might get a workplace which becomes democratized. This is all dependent on the self-interest of the person who seized the productive forces of the factory (or coffee shop).

Fantasies become powers with material backing. We see Coca-Cola plastered on a variety of surfaces. This material articulates itself due to the process of Capital, and comes into the framework of a single consciousness and produces a series of articulations and de-articulations woven through each other, throughout time. Coca-Cola is not only concerned with itself, for it must be concerned with the world in order to reproduce itself. Reality without the symptom, without the tying of rationality to self-interest, cannot understand Coca-Cola as something which is fantasy in the world, articulating itself. It is a psychological operation as well as a mechanism to accumulate money and reproduce the process of capitalism. Coca-Cola clearly through its psychological character asserts total dominance; without it, Coca-Cola is a mere curiosity. No matter how many coups it supports, it still must appear desirable. It still must put on its red dress. But it is never simply Coca-Cola itself! It is woven into the environment. A South American immigrant has a Coca-

Cola as a treat when trying to migrate north, or a cop has it in the stands of a baseball game, its universality is key to its power, and its ability to be woven into a variety of situations is key to its power.

It is crucial to the understanding of this project to know exactly how rational self-interest is not simply a singular thing within someone, but something which extends outwards into the fabric of reality, which is to say the weave which is self-interest. The ego is tied into the world, outside of itself, and thus when it knows itself as inside of itself it fails and shifts around, desperately trying to assert its disconnected nature, but also the echoes of self-interest, no longer attached to consciousnesses, litter the world as the articulated demands of the past. This failure to hold onto these things in consciousness is not unproductive. The failure of the ego to hold, and thus the creation of its symptoms, produce articulations and new fantasies, positing new registers in fantasy like the inevitable art project of simple existence.

Through the ego's failing to hold onto its creations and weaves, the objects of the Earth and the universe itself begin to articulate between each other, making the human struck through by the unintended echoes of articulated demands.

There is a key historical nature to the ego, in terms of the historical register that produces within a single person the motives and fantasies. History is thus a symptomatic engine which drives the conclusion of existential choice, and a key point of all fantasies and registers tying themselves to self-interest and rationality.

Angst is not simply a result of the ego failing, but of processes outside of the self, structural contradictions. While these subjects cannot be controlled by the ego at a single point, self-interest nonetheless in its narcissistic hubris tries to get a handle on everything, causing existential crisis for those drawn by the process of the ego which will inevitably betray itself. But the betrayal is not simply a failure of the ego failing the ego, but of the ego contradicting what is outside of a single consciousness. Ego qua ego is doomed to obscurity in its own misrecognition of its nature as something which creates and articulates outside of its own consciousness.

The negation of existential crises through rationality (which is not to say the elimination of) is able to be utilized in mental health as this process of complexity-based self-interest is revealed, rather than identifying greed immediately with self-interest. What is meaning when meaning is so multiple? Anger itself can determine itself to be righteous, painful, unnecessary, justified, but it is also multiple, an exposed nerve shining a light on something. The ego can know itself as something which escapes the singular consciousness, something which is determined by the egoic process of identification with logics, objects, other subjects, group demands, which stem from the unconscious of the person who is being crossed, and which is part and creates the world we live in.

The concept of the self-interest is worth saving and further defining. It is a fragile and rejected signifier with a spattering of poor defenders. The ignoring of self-interest, which appears at first as radical in its rejection of the greedy or dull proponents of ego, reveals itself more and more to be a source of self-aggrandizement, of course, a substance of ego and self-interest itself. This self-aggrandized ego is only the image of the ego, not the process, not its content.

The groundwork of the true content of self-interest can only begin to be known via the discoveries of psychoanalysis, and the historical logic which defines both psychoanalysis and dialectical rationality.

Part 1

Essential Properties of Psychoanalytic Self-Interest

Chapter 1

The Freudian Molecule

In dreams, fantasies emerge from a virtual space and are flung from the charged nothingness of sleep. Worlds are vividly created, worlds which are inhabited by virtual beings in a dream state which is seen as somehow less real than our conscious state. In dreams, we have not just the golden road to the human unconscious, but something which reveals the nature of reality itself, unfettered by a material neutrality. Each element in the dream makes itself present, linked with the other elements, and cut through itself by its unknown origins. The will creates the force of an articulated demand. A man may appear in a dream, but who is the man? The man is an articulated being, but not a fully formed idea. The man in the dream is a partial articulation of will, not a perfect representation, but actual in its partial articulation.

These actual appearances in their complexity and indeterminate qualities are described as molecular due to their condensing of a wide variety of ideas, trivialities, lusts, hates, worries, into what can be known as a singular item. **The formation of the singular item of fantasy is self-interest.**

The Freudian Molecule cannot be understood without knowing the dream. If we can understand this, we can start the journey into the discovery of the nature of fantasy. The Freudian Molecule in reality piles up quantitatively and forms something like a water composed of many different elements of fantasy held together in a formation of the symptom. Universal oneness in an acid-like experience can open up to us as the reality of the dream opens up. The brain no longer needs to perform a function rigorously defined by society, but only needs to dream awake to some degree. This is to say, to produce the self-interest of the singular fantasy molecule.

For example, anti-racism rushes through the world in many forms, and there is a frustration in that none of these articulations seem to rid the world of racism itself. This gap is due to the property of the fantasy not being a totality. It is actual in that it is articulated in the form of the molecule, the total of the subject which it is approaching is never totally grasped, and thus becomes only partially actualized in moments throughout history. Nonetheless a dialectical tide effecting individual psyches, laws, and power structures emerges from the primordial will toward an anti-racism.

The dislike of anti-racism's co-option by capitalism, by corporations, is a dislike of a certain molecule. As fantasy sticks to everything that is, and since capitalism is and corporations are, the formation of the corporation with anti-racism will become sticky with the fantasies of social justice, in the end to sell a product as well as to promote anti-racism. We can look at the law, as well as social application of the law, and the articulation by those in power and see how they handle anti-racism. Corporations are able to deliver anti-racism in an idealistically pure form in a sense since they do not have to be the ones who are engaging with the work of physically stopping police from killing black people extrajudicially, for instance. The police chief, who is hated as a symbol of racism, is also one who engages with the substance of anti-racism qua police power.

In a similar sense, one can see the tide of socialist signifiers as a sign of movement toward the socialist idea rather than an inevitable failure due to particular losses such as the double loss of Bernie Sanders' presidential primary runs. But what do the police chiefs think of socialism? Does it matter? The increasing quantitative tide of the socialist fantasy suggests future articulations of socialism whose actualizations in the future are still yet unknown, despite the non-articulation in the register of presidential power. We cannot understand racism nor socialism simply through the dynamic of any individual molecule or event because the most sought after force is primarily one of power in the world, rather than simple multiplicity of the fantasy which can stick to institutions. Thus, the phenomenon of power in the form of administrative control of a president or a police chief is delivered within its significance of self-interest and the multiplicity of ideas, ideas which stick to everything, and tie the world in knots.

What can be understood is that the individual instances in which racism or any other ideal become actualized within the world appear as fantasy and material. Just as in the dream, the fantasy is a purpose, but rather the field reality, in which the object of self-interest transforms in the most peculiar ways, like a chimera composed of both unconscious desires and conscious demands. There is a material police station, but there also is the fantasy which is the right of police to determine law. Like money, this functions in a highly efficient manner. No one is yelling "money isn't real! Take all of my money!" Well, some people may yell this, but they will find that their offer will be taken up quickly, since the functionality of money has material, pragmatic, and administrative consequences. One can take the money of the non-believer and go to the bank with it, and the same goes with administrative power.

The analysis of self-interest includes the escape of the fantasy into the material realm as well as the administrative, rational realm. The material realm supports the fantasy, and supports the movement of administrative control. For instance, if there is a universal interest in iron, and only one person has access to iron, self-interest will dance and form displacements of the true desire, for the technology of iron. Soon rather than being upset at the fact that one person has iron, the second person may be upset at the other for having an ugly beard in addition to control of the iron. Others will identify with the beard of the other as beautiful, but nonetheless this may be a displacement of the original necessity of iron.

If the fantasy is used to ignore the register of power, in other words, control of man, nature, environment, ideals, money, anything, then the elusive object of self-interest once again moves beyond the grasp of comprehension. Self-interest in process, which is what we are calling the Hyperstate due to its nature of being both outside the realm of consciousness, process-based, and frankly just quite large, is used to understand self-interest through the basis of fantasy. Through fantasy, control of the object is then able to be gained, control of both material and administrative power, as well as the ability to multiply the idea. One can control an iron resource and take over the world through both material wealth and rhetoric, but it can be taken back through the fantasy that one has an ugly beard, or bad mannerisms, or an inferior culture, for instance. This is the nature of fantasy and rhetoric as mapped onto material, intrinsically linked, and forever rationalized, displaced. The same goes for countries and those who are ambitious in the name of a country, the dominance of material and power is forever linked to the fantasy, and the fantasy extends into the material wealth of the country.

In Freud's *Psychopathology of Everyday Life*, Freud maps out the linguistic unconscious, and the mechanisms of forgetting and the chaotic world of replacement of one item for another with less taboo attached to it; in other words, this is the multiplicity of repression. One word becomes substituted for the next and Freud posits this is due to sexual neuroses. It becomes abundantly clear, however, that neuroses is not just for the sexual taboo, but for the cultural taboo as well.

The Interpretation of Dreams posits itself as a map of the unconscious, and insofar as it describes the condensing of various items of the psyche in the dream, it brings forward an idea totally new to dream analysis, the molecular nature of the dream image.

The Freudian hysteric, for better or worse, is the guinea pig for this investigation into the movements of the psyche and reality at large. Freud writes of a patient, "An hysterical woman identifies herself most readily — although not exclusively — with persons with whom she has had sexual relations, or who have sexual intercourse with the same persons as herself. Language takes such a conception into consideration: two lovers are 'one.'"[1] In this case, the woman becomes the fantasy object herself, and insofar as she is seeing Freud for treatment, this woman is being cured of a psychopathological formation in which the molecular fantasy structure appears self-contradictory, and thus produces angst in her psyche.

Freud attempts to treat angst by analyzing the psychodynamic movements of his patients, and intervening in these psychodynamics via interpretation and juxtaposition in order for the psychodynamics to shift in a way which alleviates psychic pain. In other words, there is a ground of anti-self-interest within the fantasy, in which the analyst intervenes and tries to create a ground of self-interest. If a woman identifies with her mother's desire for her father, but the woman dislikes her father, then structural dissonance can produce a psychic pain, and the intruding fantasy acts as a splinter. Freud is introducing logics, his ego, into the molecular formations of the patient which the patient has identified as producing angst.

Freud elucidates the fantasy molecule further with the concept of condensation, and provides us with a more thorough example within a patient's language and dreams which he gives himself freer rein to write on. On a patient for whom the word "wet" takes upon great significance in the fantasy life, Freud writes:

She remembers that in the neighboring monastery of the Three Fountains she drank a liquor made of eucalyptus by the

Trappist monks who inhabit this monastery. She then relates how the monks transformed this material and swampy region into a dry and healthful neighborhood by planting there many eucalyptus trees. The word "uclamparia" then resolves into eucalyptus and malaria, and the word "wet" refers to the former swampy nature of the place. Wet also suggests dry. Dry is actually the name of the man whom she would have married except for his over-indulgence in alcohol... The eucalyptus also refers to her neurosis, which was at first diagnosed as malaria. She went to Italy because her attacks of anxiety, which were accompanied by marked trembling and shivering, were thought to be of material origin. She bought some eucalyptus oil from the monks and she maintains that it has done her much good. The condensation *uclamparia—wet* is therefore the point of junction for the dream as well as for the neurosis [the initial dream is a man pointing to a sign on a tree which states "uclamparia—wet"].[2]

We see the patient working out self-interest through the traversing of the fantasy, creating molecules, problem solving with those molecules. The movement here, which is important for the further development of the idea of a psychodynamic and logical process of rational self-interest, must not be simply skipped over. The psyche already virtualizes material, and thinks of new ways to combine it in order to produce something that will begin the journey of how the Freudian Molecule extends past the psyche, and into the various structures of the world which asserts itself over the individual, and the social structures which determine the individual.

When protesters tear down statues, it is the motion not of law or monetary determinacy, but rather the act is primarily within the realm of traversing the fantasy in a way that adjusts the fantasy of society. It is the creation of a molecule. Socially determined movement becomes the vessel for a death drive of the molecules of the past. No longer is the fantasy of founding the American nation present, but rather the fantasy of performing an exorcism of the American nation from its sins. This is not to forget the molecules involved in power, and the question of "what does the police chief think of socialism," something so detestable because in the United States, it is a non-entity, but it would be interesting if it was not, would it not be?

The sin of slavery is seen within the lack of recognition of slavery within a confederate monument. Thus the monument is excised from the material but presence is now given to it in its absence, in its symbolic function, and the fantasy is created in a molecular event. It is through society's Freudian nature that a new solution is able to be logically deduced: society can be treated psychoanalytically, and this psychoanalytic treatment is rational. Thus the journey into rational self-interest gains its first foothold in the Freudian discovery.

To return to Freud's dreamer, we see the symptom not as a need for dryness, but as "wet." "Wet" becomes the original, primal state of being which needs treatment just as racism is the primal state of the American country in the popular societal diagnosis, but it is also the articulated need for dryness as a base upon which to build to some extent, as well as the sexual opposite of willing to have sex, willing to engage. "Dry" can mean both the conditions are and are not met, and there is a contradiction in the signifier because "dry" means both ready and not ready.

Within the "wet" an institution appears: the monastery. The monastery suggests men with knowledge, and thus the beginning of the solution to wetness in its difficulty to make civilization, a synthesis of the sexual and the non-sexual (logically, although not necessarily in the consciousness of the dreamer). There is nature, and through the engagement of nature via the placing of the monastery, or institution of the human within nature, a work to bring this nature into the realm of the service of the human begins. Within this institution is a signifier of a civilized form of wetness, "Three Fountains." The wetness begins its transformation then, from the thing which simply is the anti-self-interested ground, the ground in which all human endeavors collapse into and fail, and thus is the negation of self-interest; it is negated by the institution of wetness, "Three Fountains."

This institution by itself is no solution, however, as the institution is still something which is outside of the dreamer, just as a police department's Internal Affairs is outside of the man on the street being beaten by the police, and thus does not physically intervene during the beating.

A side note: the faithful woman's affairs which always remain internal and never articulated to an outside affair, the fear of the internal affair, the will but not the articulation. There is much contradiction in the use of the word.

The institution is end-all articulation of self-interest, as the institution is not the full hyperstate, but an element or molecule within it. The state is a molecule, or rather, a multiplicity of molecules of fantasy and material. The linkages are both rational and material. Rational insofar as logic and administrative function work to link fantasy, material in that the productive forces work in the service of fantasy, and are controlled by humans of a particular fantasy or singular logic, or even a singular signifier. "Socialism," "Republican," can bring productive forces and material into frame and view, with the simple calling of the signifier.

The institution "Three Fountains" in Freud's dreamer's psyche undertakes a task of planting eucalyptus trees. This is the beginning of the treatment which the institution undertakes, but the first task is the monastery itself, so in fact the planting is the second movement, a solution to the wetness, but also the plant contains a surplus in that it is in fact a plant, not a simple singular thing. It is a molecule. The planting of trees has a more rational form as well, eucalyptus not emerging from the signifier of wetness, but rather something which has scientifically been determined to transform swamps into ground which can then be traversed. The ideal ground of anti-self-interest has the imperative to transform, and this is actualized in by the physical ground transforming. This is not an A=A solution, as the objects contain a surplus of meaning which shift entirely the meaning of A. Here there is a gap in between consciousness and material reality which is not overcome, but rather treated to the best ability which is possible. A psychoanalytic treatment is in line with this reality and a single cognitive or cybernetic goal which is simply accomplished directly represses the surplus which is produced.

The water becomes further muddied when it is revealed that the dialectic opposite of wetness, dryness, is embroiled in the name of the man whom she was to marry named "Dry." This man, who was imposed the signifier of sobriety in process if not consciously, reacted against this signifier by drinking. Even if we ignore the likely psychodynamic process of the man, Dry's reaction against power being imposed on him by the signifier of his name, in the fantasy of the woman this is much more clear as directly related. The ground becomes dry in the dream, and self-interest is able to be achieved, even if the goal of making the man Dry, dry from drink, was not. In the end, no singular goal can be defined as the totality of self-interest, but in the fantasy, self-interest is actualized through the work of making the wet ground, the ground of anti-self-interest, into the ground of self-interest, dry ground. Dry ground which can be built upon. Her self-interest in the matter is achieved in terms of the reduction of anxiety by an elixir provided by the monks which contained eucalyptus, the tree which dried the ground.

Chapter 2

The Negativity of the Will

The will of humanity is something which contains a multitude of substantial negative properties beneath the surface of what is spoken. Material reality can be seen as a negative of psychic reality, and their combination can be said to produce something which when working together produces, eventually, what is substantially self-interest. However, sometimes the veil and the surface are one and the same, and material and rationality come together when involved in human affairs. The unarticulated molecule has a force which is not just the unconscious, but is the surplus of material as well as the surplus of the rational, it is this unarticulated or unknown force which is the will, negative to logic and language as articulated communication in an attempt for mutually recognized symbols. One states one thing, but things link to each other, and suggest other things. Here, will is the exact negative of the spoken word in that there is something moved by the words which do not fall into the category of empirical straight forward analysis.

Between positive articulated demand and the negative of will, a gap appears.

The reality of the gap is nothing new, two categories ultimately are negatives or contradict each other, but nonetheless in their interplay produce what we know as reality. Time similarly contains a gap within language which is symbolically timeless. It is shown in the Freudian free associative act of psychoanalysis which extracts words from other words. It is outside of a material time, a chronology, which can be articulated in scheduling or calendars, and can be strung through the actual, in an attempt to unify the symbolic with the material and actual. Time's multiplicity has a distorting effect, just as "dry" can mean both something which in different logics gets associated as good, bad, and neutral. The negativity of will pushes reality in a variety of manners, will is the unarticulated force of what is, or what can be, what is rational, material, both inside and outside of consciousness in the world which is strewn with molecules of fantasy.

Freud also describes negativity as an absence which contains force in *Moses and Monotheism* when describing missing traits from religions which could not stabilize. The lack of negativity in the form of the will could not be replaced by a positive representation, since the positive representation did not represent a true articulation of will, but was only concerned with the logic of itself. From Freud on a disappeared religion:

> The Aton religion had not appealed to the people; it had probably been limited to a small circle round Ikhnaton's person...It will serve a purpose if we now note several negative characteristics of the Aton religion. In the first place, all myth, magic, and sorcery are excluded from it. Then there is the way in which the sun god is represented: no longer as in earlier times by a small pyramid and a falcon, but—and this is almost rational—by a round disk from which emanate rays terminating in human hands.[3]

This negativity of will which the obscure item provides is not adequately represented by the simple representation of the sun with the sun. The sun being represented simply by a modernist-style round disk, how the sun appears in the sky, causes the representation to fail to articulate the will, which is multiple in its negativity. What appears initially as the irrational is understood through the negativity of will as a molecule which articulates multiple primordial desires, or wills which are not yet articulate, or wills are articulated already through demand and the demand, causing more will to be created for the thing, creates more unarticulated will. Here we can rationally analyze that if we were to start a religion, or join a religion, one would have to some extent excuse the irrational aspects of the religion by virtue of rationality, unless that religion is being posited as rational unity itself. If for some reason an atheist wanted to create a religion and make it in line with basic ethical commandments, he might find himself not in line with the demand of religion itself, which is to provide a mystical, deeper reality, as well as posit points of control at times in the form of dieties (relieving the anxiety of the radical opposite of a great controller). In other words, through rationality we can rationally understand when exactly we need to discard rationality, and why. If the attempt is to participate in a pleasurable religious experience, rationality must be discarded. I prefer not to participate in such things directly, typically.

When politics takes on religion and tries to integrate it into its practice, it cannot help but be mystical and obscuring. It cannot be understood rationally as the most important force which binds together a movement. To give carte blanche to populist will is to give in to the religious impulse, which is the demand for obfuscation and mysticism itself. We can note the nature of rational inquiries, and the negative will of narcissistic participation. Humans participate narcissistically when their wills are a reflection of immediate validity rather than engaging with the universal which it is supposed to engage with. For instance, if my politics is that of an immediate demand, which I immediately assess as valid, it cannot be said to be a universal politics. This is negated, however, when immediate participation is given immediate validity, such as in some feminisms or in racial activism which attempts to include the voices of minority populations, much to the chagrin of those who wish for a politics of non-vitalism which engages always with universal laws and implications.

It is not exactly news that ideology carries with it a driving force of an idea through the world in ineffective or superficial ways, but it must here be revisited and perhaps expanded upon during the analysis of rational self-interest exactly what is the function of these "virtue signals" or acts of protests.

A basic academic example: is it in the self-interest of the person who takes the class off track for his "rational" statement, is the rational statement really worth saying, and does its relevance really determine its self-interest property? Insofar as existence is an existential choice, there is no totally correct answer, but the beginning of understanding the existential choice is the understanding of the elements. There is something wrong with this action in that the speech is not simply to answer a question, but to provide information for the class. If it provides information for the class, then there is the question of form and symbolic necessity. What is the disruption representative of?

Disruptiveness can be cited as proof of the superficiality of its claim, but of course the history of activism requires disruption, and disruption must emerge as primarily for the good rather than for the interest of one to speak or any other petty reasoning. The will hints at its nature during articulation, and is sorted into the symbolic logic of articulation. This is the difficulty of speech, how will it articulate its desire?

Disruption appears as a "burp," or as a moral necessity. Either way, will is bubbling to the surface. In reality, the extension of this disruptive burp into the world exists as material as well as will, but nonetheless humanity quickly weaves the various wills and desires into the material event.

This petty bit of will can help us understand where this negative "burp" appears in other places. The pandemic can be said to resemble a Lovecraft horror monster beneath the ice in that beneath the surface of any interaction lies the possibility of death, although at a certain point this seems to be too much psychologically for people, and people prefer the possibility of a material death to a Lovecraft reality. Death emerges from the depths to assert its existence through the virus. In the same way which we cope with death, the virus is coped with, and can be removed from the ego. This does not, of course, negate the material of the virus. The virus, like the Lovecraft monster, promotes a horror story, and thus some people choose to live in other stories, other fantasies.

Both Freud and Lovecraft map negativity as a substantial force which creates worlds and defines fantasy, but Lovecraft can be said to map the substantial elusive nature of self-interest as a Freudian Molecule, something which contains both wonder and death, in its expansion. To be in line with material, the horror narrative cannot be simply rejected when death emerges to assert its existence, unless the will to stay alive is itself negated.

Lovecraft's descriptions are image heavy and narrative-linear, and the stories work to form a descriptive process of ambiguous force which melts what was the world before and expands in a multiplicity of death as it becomes more and more definite.

There is an abstract death, which through its effect becomes more and more definite, more wonderful as well as more monstrous. In other words, it is a large, slow process of a material will, articulating. The Lovecraft story partially articulates the material will, which has a crushing or articulating of a vague artistic sensibility, if not what one could call consciousness itself:

All the farm was shining with the hideous unknown blend of colour; trees, buildings, and even such grass and herbage as had not been wholly changed to lethal grey brittleness. The boughs were all straining skyward...It was a scene from a vision of Fuseli, and over all the rest reigned that riot of luminous amorphousness, that alien and undimensioned rainbow of cryptic poison from the well—seething, feeling, lapping, reaching, scintillating, straining, and malignly bubbling in its cosmic and unrecognizable chromaticism.[4]

The conscious observer gawks at the destructive power of the blight. The material blight can provoke aesthetics in the negation of aesthetics itself, the field turning gray.

In the wake of death we see the will toward life and health begin to become more articulated along with the destruction, with the blighting of it. *Radically opposite ideals are held within a single articulation. This creates a cognitive dissonance of the material which can be seen as a key element of the horror.* Health also takes on a character similarly to those who ignore the outbreak, and a vitalism of masklessness is posited.

There seem to be plenty of people on the maskless vitalism side of the social contract. At work, the boss all but states, "We don't really have to care about COVID, do we?" I was initially told not to wear a mask during March 2020, that the material safety of the mask was actively harming the aesthetic calmness we can provide to clients. But power ultimately decides which fantasy will be replicated. The material forces of capital and the wage labor system already determined which fantasy was important; the fantasies of those who control these systems can to various degrees impose the fantasy of death-drive vitalism on others

If there were an enforcement of COVID laws in the United States, or perhaps even a basic wish to keep things closed, it might be easier for many to stay indoors. Due to the fantasy of the president and others in powerful administrative positions who are also in capitalist class positions of expanding wage labor under their control and accumulating money, the fantasies which relate to their self-interest become predominant.

We come to see this not simply as a blank existential choice which is outside of the realm of both society and rational, scientific social caution. I am socially determined by my surroundings, and yet I am enjoying the failure of the social structure. I feel free, the true American ideal, the general "Free." This fantasy has been provided for me, or rather, its molecular form has appeared linked with power.

I sit down in a Georgian dumpling place, excited to be able to be at the new restaurant. The restrictions were not simply a negation of even a vessel to this sudden enjoyment. The enjoyment provided by the restriction of the state, the restriction of the state given universal validity through the threat of imminent death.

In the negative of the ordering of a dumpling in June 2020, lies enjoyment here-to-far unknown in June 2019. Now there is only me and the dumpling of death, and it is delicious. The presence of the absence of my past relationship, the presence of the absence of the mask. In this restaurant I must eat with no mask, I can partake in the forbidden form: the maskless social person.

One would have to structurally cancel the enjoyment of others in order to work toward a will-toward-health. The ground for the battle of wills is set, but it is not simply a matter of individual choice, but something which requires a fight over what becomes articulated. There is no simple peace between wills, no Absolute non-competition, because the fantasy and the ego are also the material reality which is outside of individual consciousness. One can, however, recognize the limit of their acts. As of July, my value of safety has won out over the perverse will to be eating in restaurants without a mask, and I haven't been to a restaurant to sit down without a mask in a while.

I don't bring this example to posit the mask debacle, the great culture war as the war which ends all wars, but it is the clearest example of fantasy and material coming together to articulate into a material creation to counter another material. The mask counters the virus, there is an idea behind this as well as material. On the second front of this war, there is a battle to determine if a mask contra virus materialism is really necessary.

Fantasy becomes tied in a knot, and power and material determine which fantasy moves back into the consciousness, and creates consequences and manufactures desire, and forces one into various positions on health.

The negative of the will lays the ground for the conflict of the positivity of the demand. This is the exact place we must start to get into the conflict of wills which extend past the single consciousness, and material comes into conflict with not only other material, but the absence of itself. The mask material is in conflict not only with the virus, but it is in conflict with its own absence.

Chapter 3

The Positivity of the Demand

The ideas of mankind contain a surplus in their appearance. Through the domain of language and idea, fantasy undergoes a transformation. While fantasy has the property of being created with origin points in psychoanalytic fantasy, it is able to transform and be analyzed rationally through its own understanding, and determined to have an essential property. Here, its own understanding takes the form of something which posits itself to be an empirical singularity. The self-reflective singularness of purpose reflecting rationality allows for transformation of the will into something different, something which can be then articulated into something which can be worked through logically, allowing the ignoring of the unconscious, the cognization of reality away from its primordial origins. What was a hysteric character in negative space enters the realm of speech and human communication and allows for a singularity of purpose; the birth of cybernetics comes from the denial of multiplicity.

When states become involved, universality idealism quickly folds to the weave of demands which counteract each other, and power, material in the form of trade goods, and alliances come into play; alliances which have to do with, what else, alliances, power, and material goods. Let's take mid-nineteenth century France for example:

The law of the 16th of July aggravated the severity of the press restrictions by re-establishing the "caution money" (cautionement) deposited by proprietors and editors of papers with the government as a guarantee of good behavior. Finally, a skillful interpretation of the law on clubs and political societies suppressed about this time all the Republican societies. It was now their turn to be crushed like the socialists, But the president had only joined in the Montalembert's cry of "Down with the Republicans!" in the hope of effecting a revision of the constitution without having recourse to a coup d'etat. His concessions only increased the boldness of the monarchists; while they had only accepted Louis Napoleon as president in opposition to the Republic and as a step in the direction of the monarchy. A conflict was now inevitable between his personal policy and the majority of the Chamber, who were, moreover, divided...[5]

The socialist critique of the weapon being more important than the weapon of critique is apparent here. The socialists, republicans, monarchists, and Bonapartists all competed and utilized each other for their own ends, but eventually it was the Bonapartists who would come out on top.

Speech and word appear from humanity in the form of logic but they also represent the material and power realities of those logics. The fantasy becomes articulated and equivalencies are laid onto each faction, as hierarchies of dominance are established. Despite being unpopular, Napoleon III was able to rise through power due to the power behind the idea of power itself. It does make some sort of intuitive logic that those who demand a source of ultimate authority and power would be able to exact such an ultimate authority and power, making the anti-authoritarian task of dividing authority difficult in its disunity.

Whatever the origin of the unconscious and the conscious properties of the original will, the will's articulation makes will determinate and posits itself, lacking its original pre-articulated properties. Through speech and language, will becomes demand, and language appears not as a descriptor or a vessel, although it is both, but as the key method for the transformation of will into the space of what is shared humanity. The two people who ally for power may ultimately serve in a single articulated positive form, but for two completely different ideological reasons, ideology being the gap between the unconscious will and the positive demand.

Time takes on an Actual character and is no longer simply transcendental within Freudian consciousness, which is to say, words no longer appear non-chronologically in order to make the returned of the repressed (or just a return of the previous and relevant), but rather through language a second point is reached, which is not a point at all but a secondary movement, in its multiplicity. All "nows" of the world become second movements as all actualities reveal themselves and posit their own existence. Now, not being explicitly human is dirempted from demand due to the linguistic necessity of demand. Napoleon III contains within him the power of Napoleon I in this manner, which is transcendental/psychological, but nonetheless functions in order to give this one specific man, in a highly contested region, power. The "now" contains within it the past, which is psychoanalytic and associative in nature.

To reverse course, we can move from demand back to Will to find primordial connections. Will, once it is known as something Freudian, rather than something of a Bonapartist conquest, the lower-case popular notion of will, can be thoroughly investigated in a richer manner. The movement of demand back into will is thoroughly charted by the psychoanalyst's movement toward the opposite, the bringing of will into the space of speech, into the realm of the demand, in that it is the reversal of will's movement into repression and spoken back to articulate what was half-thought. Psychoanalysis through language has the property of generating demand articulations in the register of speech, allowing the space to move from a vulgar and unarticulated preconscious state.

The idea of a "triumph of the will" would only be a movement which was purely directed toward becoming-primal. It is no wonder that the fascist or monarchist tendency tends toward anti-peaceful ideals, toward power unchecked by law through its lack of adversaries. Strange that the man who oversaw the Pogroms, Alexander the III, via Wikipedia, was also known as the "peacemaker." Peace, of course, is not the "natural state" itself within which a will fetish is fully articulated, but rather the movement toward primal pre-verbal articulations, the will for a single point of control moved into gods and men who act as gods of lands. The movement of a man toward the murder of another man, or the violence of conflict and the fetish of power appears as a move toward anti-rationalism, anti-articulation of rational principles which counter the single point of control.

Animals themselves can be said to be creatures of unarticulated will so long as they do not have language, but that is not something which I can prove. Animals may have a rudimentary system of language, and through this language rational self-interest through articulation and disarticulation is possible.

Thus we find ourselves at the point where we can define rational self-interest, as it reveals itself to be the historical movement of articulation and disarticulation fluctuating between negative Will and positive Demand, stuck through with fantasy and lacking a singular "point." Not a cybernetic goal or end, but rather a fluctuation between articulations and disarticulations, between the positive and negative.

The historical movement of Demand and Will is not the transcendental Freudian time where fantasy boils from, the negative space of Will, but rather the rationally understood movement of language and its conglomeration into total Being. In other words, rational self-interest as the real movement which contains transcendental and historical properties both transcends and becomes actual through time. The fourth dimension is dirempted and split into transcendence and actuality, transcendence being the primordial space, and actuality being the space of articulation.

Cast Away

Initially, Tom Hanks cares about his job at Fed Ex and managing postal workers to be an efficient force. He plans to get married to a woman he loves. Things are going smoothly for Tom.

Then, of course, the event which defines the film. The plane crashes and now he is on an island with the help of a raft. Once he is on the island, the items change in character. Packages now become lacking possibilities of rescue, of life. His materials slowly break. The lightbulb in the flashlight that he pulls off the dead captain. His leg injury, which could be taken care of quite easily in a hospital at home, takes on a menacing, questioning character.

In simple terms, the systemic shift absolutely changes the character of the objects. "The most beautiful thing in the world is of course the world itself," reads one of the birthday cards. "The world on time," reads the front of a FedEx package. Messages take on a dreamlike character once they are removed from their original context, which is the dull, every day. These messages were not un-dreamlike before, but once removed from the mundane they take on the character of the surreal.

After Tom Hanks smashes his tooth out with an ice skate, we are suddenly transported 4 years into the future. Experience lends him increased skills in surviving in the material system that he has been jolted into. His volleyball friend Wilson's hair lengthens.

Tom Hanks is brought back to the civilized world to find that crab is easily accessible, and fire comes on with the flick of a switch.

There are three distinct phases here. Tom is pre-event, in the day-to-day routine. Secondly, Tom comes face-to-face with the event, has limited experience, and is thrust into the role of the novice. Third, Tom gains expertise in the new material situation that he enters into, and decides to escape it. Finally, he is back in civilization, a man thrown from his horse and sitting on it again.

Tom articulates getting back together with his love, Kelly, who has married another man. They kiss and begin to drive off as if they are running away. Tom then pulls back into the garage and there is a mutual agreement that the urge should be sublimated and that they have fidelity to the way things are. The loss becomes concretized. As Tom continues his fourth stage journey into civilization, he delivers a package which he says saved his life to an empty door. As he leaves, a woman says he looks lost and flirts with him as Tom stands in the middle of a crossroad. As she drives away, her truck reveals that she was the person who sent the package that saved his life, with the same wing logo on her truck that was on the package. Tom smiles at being flirted with, the linking between his material savior and la femme, abstract possibility opens up, and the credits roll.

Gladiator

Roman General Russell Crowe begins by defeating an army and revealing that he just wants to farm. Before Russell can manage this, the emperor castrates his son who mingles in a bourgeois manner, asking the anachronistic small talk question of "emperor or senate" to the would-be farmer Russell Crowe.

Then the emperor announces to the Tom Bradyesque, down-to-earth Russell Crowe that he embodies the values. He is an innocent, like Alice who visits Wonderland, but unlike Alice, the innocent represents the highest ideal of the symbolic order rather than the symbolic order's radical questioning. Innocence takes on the feature of a potentiality for a greater symbolic order, but of course since innocence is simply the absence of knowledge, the failure of this ideal is saved by the killing of the emperor.

Soon Russell Crowe is "The Spaniard" and all he has is his infinite ability to defeat anyone in battle which comes his way. While *Gladiator* won the academy award and "Cast Away" did not, something is missing here. The infinite ability to defeat others, and the innocent archetypal sports star defeats the petty emperor who questions the republic and references "the people."

In this story, something is revealed, however. The interest in the greatness of the people's warrior over the people's superficial representative. The people's warrior must be punished unjustly, while the superficial representative be rewarded unjustly. The entire set up of "Gladiator" is to reveal a fictional Christian warrior. Not a Christian in the religious sense, but a consistent moral innocent, who defeats all in his path with his Christian values.

He spits into the crowd after doing their bidding, and the crowd loves him for it. He is their antithesis.

In Rome, he is no longer the antithesis, he is one with the crowd as he reveals himself to be the savior of the ideal emperor who would be the founder of the republic, in an extraordinary fidelity to ahistorical idealism where Aurelius didn't rule with Commodus and was instead murdered by him.

In these situations, events which are outside the individual radically change the nature of demand, and demand is shown as purely conditional, and in the sense of something whose negative is the general will and desire of its subjects, a positive content which takes the shape of a variety of forms. The appearance of their forms is not universal, but is the positive content of self-interest. **Self-interest reveals itself to be two-fold: conditional and determined by time, as well as in the forms of objects in the world.**

Self-interest is conditional in that the object is not a universal maintaining an object purity, but something which is defined by systems and material conditions. Self-interest also appears as objects, something which is sent to someone for their birthday becomes something else when Tom Hanks finds it on his "Cast Away" island.

Thus the objects of the world form a positive content, which twist and turn due to the gravitational force which is self-interest. This web forms a dreamlike quality to the world, which escapes linear understanding if one is to discover meaning in the multiplicity of reality.

Chapter 4

Ideology in Wonderland

[Alice:] 'If anyone can explain it...I'll give him six pence. I don't believe there's an atom of meaning in it.' The jury all wrote down on their slates, 'She doesn't believe there's an atom of meaning in it,' but none of them attempted to explain the paper.[6]

The articulations of self-interest are not held in the body, but present in the world as unarticulated will and positive speech. This is the simple point which must be drawn over and over when understanding self-interest's dreamlike emergence, and the condensation of various essences into a single Freudian Molecule in the world. Self-interest emerges into both material and event, which contains the surplus of multiple vectors of self-interest as well as the surplus of language itself. Two men, two self-interests within a single articulation. Thus, miscommunication becomes inscribed in the object, a gap which is the gap between meanings, contained by a single articulated demand. The gap between as well as the understanding of this gap via image and logic is fantasy, containing both the force of will and positive content as demand.

This process of understanding self-interest, or something which the self is interested in, is in itself something which is both positive and negative in content. The identifying as positive content as positive, or negative content as negative, feeds the conscious the world that it will integrate into its own history. Identity contains its own nothingness in its singularity, but nonetheless contains a certain force. In psychotherapeutic treatment, the identification of someone as a diagnosis can provide an understanding of various forces through the structure of identity.

The radicality and radical conservatism of identification appears, as the identification of ourselves within the ideological framework of our surroundings allows us to enjoy and function, while an identification with one's own moral underpinnings causes a rift between ourselves and what is. Identification with what is acceptable is the ultimate conservative fidelity. Enjoyment becomes present in the positive identification and re-identification after the identity contains within it the cognitive dissonance of the previously described Lovecraft horror due to its contradiction. Identification with something radically different opens one's self up to pain. To change, one must be vulgar rather than poetic, to lose vulgarity may simply fuel the horror of the contradictions when one cannot push away from what is, to deny the agreement of identity (see Chapter 13 for more on how identity is in fact an agreement).

An identity produces a surplus of positive content and also unconscious will of the thing which one identifies as. It is an enslavement to a symbol, but this can also be a liberation. Identification contains the primordial will, which is unconscious in character and from which positive articulations spring. Identification is the negative of the non-articulated will, in that it is a positive content. As "black" one can symbolically operate through processes defined as liberatory for those who are "black." But if one is black and denies this identification, one cannot grasp what is at hand. One who is "Jewish" can enter into things designed for people who are "Jewish," such as Birthright which allows one to take a free trip to Israel, which has a logic as being good for people who are "Jewish," etcetera.

I am bored waiting for a job interview because I have showed up in the area 5 hours early because of initially being excited for a job interview. Then, when the man who owns the place interviews me and offers me money, I am excited. He is Jewish, I am also Jewish, this sameness might produce smoothness of the symbolic. I want to have a job, he wants to hire someone. Is he too Jewish for me, will he consider me not Jewish enough? I find this unlikely, my last name is highly Jewish. But to give someone a salary of a certain amount is too much for a process of one conversation, and thus a second partner is brought in. Now I am no longer bored, I am nervous. As soon as I recognize this as a natural emergence of a second individual to stem the immediacy of the initial acceptance of me into the job with which comes a salary, I am calm again. I am ready for the dream to continue, which is to say reality which bubbles up in the form of events, reality which is terribly non-linear. To call it nonsensical, or to call the man's initial acceptance of me rash, misses the immediate ethical property of self-interest as the driving force, and that driving force's nature to be molecule, surplus, non-linear, and dreamlike into its emergence into the frame of chronological time.

The poet states a variety of happenings. The poet walks up the steps, the poet sees this guy and that gal. The romantic doings of the world, the little aspects of reality from which one achieves knowledge and enjoyment. To liberate oneself from all of reality is a purely negative task, but ultimately it is simply a misrecognition about the flow of time itself.

This negation, however, is also the process of rational self-interest, the positing of something in the world. The misrecognition of reality as bubbling receives validation when a task is set and completed. Rationality allows one to reflect on one's being and adjust for self-interest, but contains within it the property of negating the self-interest itself, the self-interest being of sense and immediate material feeling, as well as a fantasy with logic. Logic can then be identified with, and reality can fade into the background. Reality's necessity of fading into the background to complete a single, cybernetic goal creates reality as something which functions as the return of the repressed. That which sneaks into the logic of the goal, or exists simultaneously of the goal, with other substantial tasks in mind.

A downhill skateboarder doesn't get rid of a helmet to lose weight in order to get down a hill faster, the two goals of not cracking one's head open and getting down the hill quickly exist simultaneously, but as the first goal is taken care of as much as possible through the material appearance of a helmet, it is forgotten to some extent, and becomes integrated with other manners into the goal of getting down the hill quickly. Safety becomes intuitive, while speed becomes more in the forefront, tempered by safety by the expert. For the new rider, this may be reversed, and safety is at the forefront due to it not being intuitive, and speed may become totally irrelevant or even a burden.

The gap appears between the two positive engagements of the goal and the human with its Freudian nuances, and this gap is an essential property of being which in part produces the virtual object of rational self-interest. Both are arbitrary, neither are an Absolute of any kind, even if the one posits itself as more essential than the other. The goal states the psyche is tenuous, the psyche knows the goal as singular and foolish. It is an essential property of being, that these two aspects interact with each other, and are thus the exact negatives of each other in relation to self-interest. **The negative relation between psychodynamic processes and goal-based thinking and acting produces a positive content which we can call a basic substance of ideology.**

In *Alice in Wonderland*, a story is told of a girl who through her innocence and pure heartedness is able to overcome the tangled world which she is dropped into. The ideology is that of the symptom which manifests in the rational engaging of the world. Through time when a world is created, structural antagonisms manifest. The innocent, literally dropped into Wonderland, is seen as the mechanism which can save the world

Innocence does in fact pose a question to the world and

hystericizes it in the structure. The innocent is not an absolute or something to return to, in process it is the form of Socrates when he states that he does not know, and the fictions of ideology then must be repeated to someone who is not tangled in their web.

This process of reflection upon the sensory or bodily Freudian realm, which is to say rationality itself, contains within it its own nothing, the introduction of the abstract elements into the sensual. The positive or negative sensory experience of the innocent has rationality unified with it where the positive or negative sensory experience of those embedded in the world do not. Those who are interested historically in an order have their senses and their rational identification of their senses tied up with reason, and reason has tied itself with specific goals. The innocent is presumed to not have specific goals, but to only judge through senses.

The sense realm as positive or negative appeals to the personal history, the dislocated observer, and judgment becomes that of will, of primordial intuition. With the steady hand of those in the Queen's court, primordial intuition is simply a measure of cybernetic satisfaction; did Goal "A" happen or not? When Goal A is the arrest and prosecution of Alice, we are pulled toward defending the innocent who was thrown into the world and subject to the tyranny of its rulers.

In order to avoid the trap of pure idealism, which would miss the purpose of recognizing the demands within structure, we must put this rational identification back outside itself. Alice is not just Alice, but a cohort of dissidents alongside her. The fantasy of sense utility, overcoming the order of what is, is achieved. This is fiction.

The ideology is at war with its exact negative. The legitimacy of the Queen of Hearts is at war with its exact negative, her illegitimacy. The forces at work know this, while all the while this question is never fully taken up by Alice. Alice maintains the sense-purity, there is first a measure of justice via sense, then when it is thrown into the fire of the court system, it becomes the articulation of the failure of the system itself.

The ultimate process of de-articulation, Alice's waking, comes at a time where it seems that the system is coming down on her. The system is shown to have no material worth but is merely phantasms in which Alice has reality, and the phantasms do not.

Alice's dream can be understood as the process of self-interest. Molecules appear to her of various fantasy qualities, which appeal to different wishes and demands. Eventually, a demand with strong structural backing in the form of the trial participations comes into play.

But what if Alice could not wake up? The fantasy of fiction is surely the waking and dissolving of all contradiction. One does not have to become tangled in the system or engage with its contradictions due to the fact that one can always awake and de-articulate the entire charade.

When two people agree on a contract and one goes back on the contract because the terms were intrinsically exploitative, then we are in the realm of something which has a heavy amount of ideal involved. The double articulations of both what is being spoken and what is being referenced outside the two parties conjure up a whole castle of specters and phantasms all designed to pull one to the interest of the other. If they can reach a mutual agreement, and they both decide they must reach mutual agreement, then they will be subject to this battle of specters. This process extends to power, and institutions which are outside of the person. **The interpersonal expands outside of the realm of two people and translates to two substantive categories of people; the result of which is law and material power in the world.**

It is not simply a matter of power being held by a person, but power in the world having a structure which is that of a gap between its articulated purpose and its psychoanalytic movements. For instance, a purpose can be most substantially a wish, while it is being posited as a plan for actualization. Or a word can be primarily an anxiety, while it is given to be a wish. A word can be displaced, and the true articulated with can be overlooked. Or a word could be a less intense, less accurate description of something, it can be sublimated. Power too in the world can take on these processes. A labor board in the United States can function as the sublimated wish for workers to have rights, while failing to do anything but require companies who break their laws to put up posters for a few months saying that they broke the law. The demand of the company reveals itself to be stronger than the demand of the laborer in this system.

The interpersonal, the interactions between two groups of actual, material conscious people, cannot be the end of the journey of self-interest, self-interest must recognize itself in the institutions of the world which define reality. Rational identification of the surrounding world comes into play in order of the tide of a singular demand, in Alice's case, the demand of the Queen for Alice to be at the trial, taking over and destroying the multiplicity of sense-fantasy. In the real world, however, there is no waking up. The remains of the interactions between two types of people, which is to say rational singularities which are articulated as the essential quality of people, exist within the world, in the other than itself. Thus, the molecule in itself is thrown into the world, and finds articulation in that which is not purely itself, and self-interest is thrown radically outside of itself, becoming de-articulated in its original forms and goals, and rearticulated in other manners; as both antithetical notions, its own disappearance, and the reappearance of the force of itself as something which was not the isolated thing.

Finally we land upon The Ego Substance, which is the force of self-interest actualized and transforming, dialectically progressing through time and understanding through that which is not the original thing, condensing and abjecting from itself, until it can only be known as The Ego Substance which is the thing that continues onward toward various evolutions, various vectors of self-interest which are rationally known in the world and in consciousness.

Part 2

Dialectical Egoism: Vectors of Self-Interest

A: Universal Movements

Chapter 5

The Ego Substance and Articulating the Symptom

When one discusses egoism, one must talk about a usage, or the Aristotelian final cause, the use of an object. Usage, a conscious engagement with a system, is self-interest. The elements of self-interest already exist within consciousness and are articulated within the world, but the bridging of this gap is also self-interest, the actual movement of people within this gap. This final cause is something which is articulated with various purposes and materials in mind, but the gap between this and the instability of the articulation with regards to its usage is the substance of self-interest, which is to say this is an essential property of The Ego Substance. The fluctuating usage as observed through the process of time interacts not only with the purpose, but with its original intent in two different forms. Firstly, is a total and absolute deterritorialization, which is an ideal. Secondly, the original intent returns in the form of a psychoanalytic repression.

A lost object may be used in a second way, and there is an ideal of a clean break, such as the package sent in the *Cast Away* example in the third chapter. Tom Hanks becomes free of the social systems which he is in and re-arranges reality. This re-arrangement is framed not as a gain but an obvious tragedy, the tragedy of being marooned on an island with no means of escape. For Tom the symptom is immediately obvious: "I am stuck on an island and I want to leave it!" Thus his self-interest is to leave the island, while also surviving on the island long enough to leave it.

In *Gladiator*, another fiction, the symptom is easily known. His family have been killed, and now he wants revenge against the evil emperor, which he then gets. A simple symptom, but trauma is often simple but unable to be articulated. It also invigorates him to do other glorious acts, such as use his ability to defeat all who take him on at hand-to-hand combat.

From my own hysteric engagement with mental health: a symptom was that I didn't think mental health care helped me all that much, and I wanted to find out why. I became a therapist and read a lot of philosophy and psychology. Through these articulations and the force of the other, I became for mental health, where initially I was not for mental health, I was only for myself. Thus, the appearance of mental health now took on a very different form.

Mental health, however, in order for it to be for the other, and thus in-and-for itself through the helping of the other, must engage with the other that is not engaged with it. Thus a superegoic tension is created.

A relationship can explain tension in the framework of self-interest as symptom identification.

A relationship ending, split from the relationship, and split from the desire of himself as well as the desire of the other, creates a chasm in The Ego Substance, and the unity breaks apart into things which are no longer in-and-for themselves, and thus a crisis comes in the forcing of what was articulated in the form of a relation and back into an individual.

Through my own hysterics, which I am very familiar with, I can serve as an example of the shift in self-interest and the detaching through an exit, and the difficulties within:

I miss her so much, I hate that it had to be like this. But it did have to be like this, I could bear the angst no longer. I hate that I see it as a symptom, and thus I dislike myself. Am I wrong? Do I need a cognitive reframe? Some people say, "People grow apart."

This de-articulates the symptom certainly. The symptom of mine is mostly a failure of morality, I did not live up to my own moral standards, I was weak to hold onto someone and then release them when I was less weak. An act of patheticness. I accept this as an act of patheticness. The symptom is that I am a pathetic subjectivity by my own definition.

To let go of the partner is not just to let go of the partner, since the desire of the other exists within one's own desire. The desire for the other is the desire in-and-for-itself, which is to say desire articulated in the world rather than simply held in consciousness.

Interestingly, my hysteric declaration that "I miss her so much," when I further examine it, is a feeling that she misses me, or that she wants to be with me. The Ego Substance is still aligned in the past relationship, desire being both in the world and internal creates the world as something internal. Thus the "I" which is missing her so much, is in fact her, missing me. The desire of the other is my desire within self-interest.

Secondly, positive content, the thought that I am pathetic. I lash out at myself. Do I think it is pathetic to be in the relationship? Certainly if I was to enter the relationship now I would think the casual, not thought out entrance would be somewhat pathetic. But it was articulated at a time where I didn't think this was bad, and I didn't know what I wanted in a relationship, but I only knew I wouldn't be marrying her or having kids with her, and I told her so.

Now I would not be in a relationship which couldn't be turned into such an arrangement, something I was extraordinarily invested in. This is my ideal, to have a sort of ideal love where I am invested and there is a force of will to back that conscious investment. To articulate that I am pathetic misses the necessity of the original molecular formation of the relationship, as well as the honest discussion regarding the nature of a relationship. By my current standards, I was pathetic at one point, but through that I discovered the ideal which I have now, and thus defined the past as pathetic. If I was a less pathetic man then I would be someone else now, I would have formed different ideals. If I was less pathetic, I may be more aesthetic to myself in the past.

So what I defined in the past as pathetic transcends to the present, and thus my identification with the past self as pathetic, the past self as me, I identify myself as not pathetic.

But in actuality, I guess I am not so bad...now. By my standards now. Which required the previous articulation of a relationship into the current ideal of a relationship. This is the nature of The Ego Substance, to transform in content, sublating the self, while differentiating the self within time via the ideals.

Chapter 6

Egoism as Entrance and Escape

The Ego Substance transforms, and rationally known relations of things, bound by material, behavioral, and ideological frameworks, come together and fall apart.

Self-Interest is something which escapes from what is not in its self-interest, which is the other. But the other defines self-interest in its opposition to The Ego Substance as it is in a specific moment in time. There is the existence of something which cannot be recaptured permanently, but it is nonetheless recaptured by the gravity of the motive of self-interest.

In a relationship, there are multiple goals which are rationally identifiable which one can pay fidelity to. Holding the relationship together is the highest good, as well as having a good relationship is the highest good. When these two forces interact, it can lead to a relationship which is worked on, but doesn't end up qualifying as a good relationship by standard in the future, thus de-articulating the relationship.

The forces within the movement of the human are corrosive, but they simultaneously build the entirety of the human sphere of knowledge and experience. The relationship was entered into, the relationship was exited.

Similarly, the Soviet Union was created, then it fell apart. To see a world power fall apart and my personal life encountering an event such as a relationship ending might seem to link the world-historical to the trivial, but they are both movements of The Ego Substance.

This movement of articulation of the structure speaks to an idea being fulfilled, and due to internal inconsistencies with purpose, the structure de-articulates, freeing the ideals to be recaptured by other systems, for better or worse.

The psychedelic fantasy bubble corrodes.

The dream is a system which is articulated and is satisfying to its purpose, and is thus a liberation which is an entrance, rather than an escape from a symbolic order, which is a barrage of restrictions as well as positive possibility.

Articulating an ideal within a country will be doomed to contradiction due to the multiplicity of demands on the country from inside, demands which are absolutely in contradiction with each other. The political interest group contains different motivations, but they come together and pass some law, or contain some phrase which binds them. The image creates the law, the force of the masses to create a singular goal.

This is only one interest group. The interest group fights within itself, and it fights with other interest groups. Community is stricken with a contradiction of demands.

Knowledge enters the fray, and the validity of knowledge. A subject-supposed-to-know know-how comes in the form of persons who make general morality intelligible, but then there is also knowledge of the system, subject, or particular subjects, which vie for validity. In other words, they view for the right for their knowledge to be deemed useful within an interest group, or just a group which is interested in something.

But these are persons, and persons use knowledge to wield power, ascribe worth to themselves or even with the benefit of the doubt, the world, but this is no reason to take them very seriously at all. Insofar as these persons who wield the ideal deftly into the symbolic order, they are not the fantasies themselves. Thus, they beg to be rebelled against once again, once they fail to pay fidelity to the full fantasy, which is impossible of course.

Self-interest thus reveals itself to have an essential element: an ideal of an anti-hypocritical position, and is the only rationalist position possible which has the potential to fundamentally work through its contradictions. This includes the position of

Antigone, which is the irreconcilable difference, understandable in that unitary phrase "irreconcilable difference." In this unified form, it lacks contradiction since it is contradiction.

Self-interest, through the unconscious will, captures moments of time as articulations of its logic. As molecular units of fantasy, certain events cannot be understood as the sum total of its parts, simple self-interest. Some moments can be best understood as trauma, and in that Lacanian sense what is the Real which escapes imagination and narration, a police officer beats a man in his self-interest, and the man's self-interest who is beaten is so shut off, and he is so unable to articulate his will to survive or stop the beating, the beating is then imprinted on him as something absolutely negative, something to avoid.

However, just like any object, we can take apart and examine the nature of the molecules in order to grasp a certain understanding of the item of self-interest at play, and note the differences between these molecules which to some extent attempt to create a logical extension of an idea in the world, which becomes the vessel of the interactions of principle and power. One cannot dream of the lofty machinations of long stretches of time without understanding the key molecules at play. The man being beaten by the police officer doesn't have the privilege of his principles determining the material events, while the police officer can articulate his principles in that moment, traumatizing the beating victim.

Right or law, when separated from morality, becomes nothing more than despotic duty. A man should accept his traumatic beating as simply good? No. This is duty which no longer holds the consequence of its formation, but becomes duty in itself. This is especially true in its ideal form, where Right may not even be Right at all, but the suggestion of what should be Right. It is a matter of power, not of the principle of upholding law. The man doesn't stop the beating because he either can't, or the consequences of stopping the beating would be too great.

Should the principled be doomed to become neurotic? Or is the neurosis or morality or principle extended in fact simply more refined self-reference and escape? Or is it further inside less freedom, further into non-rational obscurity?

Another coerced but not mandatory duty: in America, you are encouraged to vote.

Why do people vote if their vote doesn't count? There is power to be had when a certain quantity of people vote, but a single vote rarely has power. Duties become ridden with self-contradiction insofar as they were positing that the duty would make the principle actual, where in fact a different course to actualize the principle in the world could be taken instead. When the moral principle reflected by the duty becomes ignored or missed significantly by the duty, this duty becomes self-defeating; in other words, despotic duty.

The packing together of empty duties, half-baked consequences, simple prejudices, all baked together into what passes itself off as the man's inevitable achievement, which is then used to articulate a command upon a person. This command is wielded by both institutions and thus we gain the birth of the superego.

Chapter 7

Superego as a Unity

The Ego Substance enters into systems with contradictory aims within it. It is not only aligned with contradiction itself, but at times the impossible overcoming of contradiction in the form of two abstractions losing all definition in a single abstraction. While it is possible to have a concrete moment to in some ways "resolve" the antithetical abstractions, the unity itself contains contradiction, and that contradiction can be known as superego.

The imperative to both exit and entrance can exist simultaneously within a moment, and thus we are given discontent, which is to say the birth of the superego in the form of angst. The superego is a guide to navigate the symbolic order, but it can be trapped as a simultaneous imperative to do and to do-not. Going back to the appearance of the world in molecular condensations, or Freudian Molecules, we have a symptom of being, which is that the unity of contradiction produces angst.

Power over symbolic actions which are posited as things which move a larger object is in antagonism of a person or counter-hegemonic system which wants to escape the system for a better system. Insofar as this counter-hegemony would be catastrophic if universalized, this counter-hegemonic action would also be against the categorical, or something which should be taken by all humans in a similar situation. A good will which contains objectively, something which is a duty ethic, is in fact something which inscribes someone into hegemonic order.

Insofar as people acting in their self-interest is ethical, and angst is produced through actions which meet the qualification of the categorical imperative as well as do not meet the categorical imperative, one must have some sense of what constitutes the self to make the choice of which to engage with. Here the self appears as having interest in contrast or in congruence with the universal demand. The unity of the universal and the particular can result in the particular winning over the universal supposed "good." To state one can escape the self for the universal posits the superego unity of the particular and the unity, and the kingdom of ends becomes a kingdom of angst and discontent.

To align fully with law and ideology is the ultimate superegoic act, to become a zealot is to be a unifier. When subjectivities are counted up one by one, and we see how many proudly call for the death of others in the name of a national duty. This is of course against a general dislike of death, for many. One can take up their symbols and call them the state symbols, one can even take the state law and call it the state itself, but insofar as any particular law represents the state, the state can never be grasped as it is a failing ideal, something which posits a morality and good will but ultimately is split from that morality and good will. What is left is the symbolic surplus of actions.

The superego is created when a unity is created between opposites, a structural superego. There is a unity in a word and its function, events, molecular appearances, and in logics. The surpluses are then dealt with in various manners: repressed, cast aside, or sublated into further defining the unity, or understood as irrelevant. A sort of skate is created through the process of identification with narratives, logics, and cybernetic functions of control.

Chapter 8

The Negative Power of Myth

The Ego Substance contains a negative force of will that may obscure itself through various means.

The positive demand takes on the form of both logic and the surreal. One might even say myth is the more effective vessel of the demand, because it contains within it camouflage, less friction for its demands. Structures both have and attempt to determine, and so do people. Reason qua reason allows one to see the features of a structure, when one engineers a building, one wants to know the material one is working with, what will stand, what will not stand. Within architecture there is another aspect, which is the general molecular quality of the building or space. A house contains both reason and myth, and is built upon both.

A system of power, an apparatus, must contain both myth and reason. The myth of reason is that reason contains no mythic powers, and it becomes linked to a variety of empirical facts, linked by the fantasy of pure anti-myth. The structure is unable to incorporate the truths of myths because of the veneer of fiction which myths contain, but nonetheless the myth contains within it the logic of the molecular demand. In Chapter 2, The Negativity of the Will was shown to provide a wider range of demands when in the form of a sun god rather than a minimalist representation of the sun.

This does not make myth immanently good, but it does speak to the power of myth. Myth can carry with it a variety of various demands within its structure since its fictional tale doesn't take the form of the positive logical proposition, which is the negative will articulated as clearly as possible, creating a surplus of its own failure to do so exactly. The mythic structure allows, for instance, for the politics of the day to be integrated with something like personal hygiene, like in the example of Jordan Peterson who provides myths which have angered many for their integration of mental health with conservative politics. Whether or not the mental health advice is sound or not, the mythic form which integrates conservative talking points, the unity between mental health and conservatism, provokes the ire of those who do not want the conservative superego present within mental health.

The state, being a unity, contains the property of being intrinsically a superegoic structure. The structure provides guidance, but it has a second quality of internal dissonance. The internal dissonance, as a gap between positive contents of demand as well as psychoanalytic contents of will, is a breeding ground for ideological specters of all kinds to grow. If we are to take one's own self-interest and posit it as the ground of being, then self-interest is also the gap between interests. A substance of being is this gap between interests, and the dissonance between interests.

The myth obscures these gaps and allows for functioning through a supposed unity, which in fact paints over the contradictions of the logical demand quality of demands which are made. A demand for communism contains both the demand for recognition of racism qua racial difference and a lack of racism qua racial difference within a single group, but the myth of communism can paint over this absolute Antigone and carry forth other concrete demands, and this makes the myth carry people who may have opposite demands in the direction of a unitary goal.

In Hegelian terms, the abstract ideals of both, the negation of their absolute opposition, and the concrete creation of a goal. The goal, as something which creates a psychoanalytic gap, may itself then create symptoms with the achievement of itself, insofar as the absolute contradiction of the unity creates antagonism which is determined to be negative.

Chapter 9

The Hyperstate's Relation to Myth

The Ego Substance aligns with reason and decoding in order to make apparent power in the world, to either know it, enact it, or act against it with a clarity.

The Hyperstate is the totality of the intrinsic logic of self-interest, and thus it is specifically contrary to myth's tendency to an anti-rational view. However, insofar as myth is the articulation, an actual positive demand, myth is in fact an articulation of the Hyperstate. The Hyperstate as the actual movement and force of self-interest through its articulations and de-articulations makes myth its radical opposite, which is the pushing of the actual movements into the background, while the Hyperstate pushes movements into the foreground. However, because myth can also reveal logic, the myth is a higher, negative articulation of the Hyperstate. It is the negativity of will, articulated in fiction.

Contrary to Myth, the reason for the existence of the Hyperstate is not simply because of the demand for rationality qua the demand for rationality, but because it is a map of a causal, gravitational force. This is to say, there are things which are able to be done through rationality, and there is also the desire for rationality itself, and when things are articulated and removed from the form of the myth and into the form of its actual self-interest content, this is aligned with the movement of rationality insofar as it shows the self-interest content within event. This removes the mystique of myth for analysis of the movement of its dialectical forces.

This is not to say the myth does not contain rationality. For two oppositional forces may approach each other, and one may win the other over with a particularly moving myth which could not convince the other with simple rationality.

The Hyperstate takes the ideals of myth by positing the myth's dialectical forces, which when clear allows one to act with or radically against it. A political force which operates through myth can be analyzed through the Hyperstate. Is Trump lying, or is he achieving lines of logic which would be forbidden by dominant ideologies? It is both, but to simply state he is lying in any particular case misses the motivation for the lie, and the ideological reason that the lie is articulated in the way it is.

Rationality can then create a poor judgment where the function of the myth is obscured. The creation of an absolute truth, or something posited as pure rationality, misses its surplus and its excess. Many times within casual discourse, however, this simple form must exist, and absolute truth must be posited, knowing full well it is not enough. This leads us back to the substance of ideology as the gap between goal and the negative content of will outside of the articulated foal.

Right-wing thinker Nick Land loves China, but hates communism, to put it vulgarly (but efficiently). China is overtly a communist country. Ideology, myth, and poetry come alive to fill this gap:

> The Superiority of Far Eastern Marxism. While Chinese materialist dialectic denegatives itself in the direction of schizophrenizing systems dynamics, progressively dissipating top-down historical destinations in the Tao-drenched Special Economic Zones, a re-Hegelianized "western Marxism" degenerates from the critique of political economy into a state-sympathizing monotheology of economics, siding with fascism against deregulation. The left subsides into nationalistic conservatism, asphyxiating its vestigial capacity for "hot" speculative mutation in a morass of "cold" depressive guilt-culture.[7]

What religion will we worship? Have we not surpassed religion? Religion requires negative space, or it will die from redundancy. You don't need the religion if you simply have some object which is outside of religion. Religion is the negative space. Land, too, has negative space, and his religion is fueled by the power of myth and poetics certainly.

There is more than just myth, however, through the power of the negative new posits which emerge. An idea of two communisms, not of Mao's capitualting and non-capitualating communism, but of a Chinese versus western Marxism, with Chinese "materialist dialectic" being a machine fueled by its multiple economic areas and its challenging of "systems dynamics," while western Marxism is the unity of depression, guilt, and conservatism.

Sartre takes a more explanatory tone when arguing or explaining why God is not all it seems. In comparison to land, there is something commonsensical about Sartre stating something that doesn't challenge the current order, besides maybe conservative readings of God. Sartre de-mysticizes:

The link between transcendence as constitutive of man (not in the sense that God is transcendent, but in the sense that man passes beyond himself) and subjectivity (in the sense that man is not an island unto himself but always present in a human universe) is what we call "existentialist humanism."[8]

Here the functions of God as multiple are decoded qua the decoded, but they are not recoded immediately as something else. They are given the label of humanist, which speaks to man as one who has needs, needs which are fulfilled by the God myth. To speak of things in terms of humanistic needs rather than self-interest, however, limits the God myth.

For instance, there can be the interest to kill which the God myth fulfills. This interest of killing is not a humanism. The choices within Sartrean existentialism discuss moral dilemmas and duties to other human beings, but this is a myth with the demand for a duty toward other human beings. To further decode the God example, one can easily look at the Catholic Church, where God myths function to molest boys, or American soldiers, where God and Country in a unity combine to drive one to duty overseas, or the obvious suicide bomber who blows themselves up through the God myth.

Decoding allows us to lay bare the truth of the demands: to un-sublimate them. When they are revealed, they may or may not function. To de-mystify is not always a moral actor within the interest of the de-mystifier.

Humanism as Sartre describes it is certainly a myth, this is a myth which Nick Land replaces with anti-humanist capitalism:

The Turing Test. Monetarizing power tends to effacement of specific territorial features as it programs for migration into cyberspace. Capital only retains anthropological characteristics as a symptom of underdevelopment; reformatting primate behavior as inertia to be dissipated in self-reinforcing artificiality. Man is something for it to overcome: a problem, drag.[9]

Both are moral posits, both are demands. The demands of Sartre appeal generally, and Sartre is held in high esteem with many. This is most likely due to the myths being in service of a common demand: serve other people on this Earth, altruism. There is a general desire to serve the other, and a myth served to articulate this desire is not very controversial.

On the other hand, Nick Land articulates a strange desire, the desire of a sort of anti-altruism, anti-"humanism." This is not to say altruism is not somewhere within Nick Land's thoughts, but the aesthetic of destroying altruism in favor of intelligence qua capitalism both posits a rational idenotification of a tendency as well as a demand which is avant-garde rather than populist. Nick Land and Sartre are playing two entirely different ball games.

As I was writhing on my bed in pain for hours in June 2020 (not due to corona but due to an osteopathic condition) shortly after I perversely enjoyed sitting down in restaurants, I couldn't help but be satisfied that I karmically deserved the pain, by my own mental unity with the command to stay at home. Here I am Sartrean, I did not serve the other enough (although I did follow guidelines!) Is this "western Marxism" at work? This is a circling of a superego, an attempt to overcome the superego which unifies. I do unify myself with humanity, and through this I have a demand at other times that other people think of other people and act in their interests to some degree, to put some effort into keeping other people alive. This is existentially arbitrary, just as doing the opposite would also be arbitrary. I choose to serve man at times, but this is superegoic.

> Kennedy had the moon-landing program. Reagan had star-wars. Clinton gets the first-wave of cyberspace psychosis (even before the film).Manned space flight was a stunt, SDI was strategic SF. With the information superhighway, media nightmares take off on their own: dystopia delivery as election platform, politics trading on its own digital annihilation.
> Nick Land[10]

This is humanism because we remind man that there is no legislator other than himself and that he must, in his abandoned state, make his own choices, and also because we show that it is not by turning inward, but by constantly seeking a goal outside of himself in the form of liberation, or of some special achievement, that man will realize himself as truly human.

Jean-Paul Sartre[11]

In July 2020, the disgust reaction regarding restaurant dining sets in for me. I use the now allowed outdoor sitting once, but there is something different in the eyes of the men and women around me this month. There is no guilt free enjoyment, there is a hostility toward the people of the outdoors now. It's a bad scene, a bad vibe. No sit-down restaurants. No eating outside. The state's control of restaurant law drastically takes an effect on my relation to the COVID19 crisis. Petty, but uncommon? I'd bet it was not unusual for a small change in the law to greatly affect the psyche of the people in the anti-authoritarian sympathizing USA.

In short: I desire to be good, but that good is in the form of an ideal. Thus, my self-interest is in the form of idealism.

B: The Good Cause

Chapter 10

Knowledge of The Good Cause

The Ego Substance passes into The Good Cause in its unity with knowledge and power, and the negative will pushing the articulations of an **ideal** through the world. Consciousness of the ideal is not merely individual, but a result of the ideal in the world, and thus power in the world becomes known to the individual, if not embodied.

An ideal is a set of tendencies known by a signifier. These signifiers have various consistencies within people, institutions, and ideals, regarding the meaning or process of the signifiers.

Myth and more direct rational articulations which align with specific goals come together and posit themselves toward a singular ideal. They are, however, a multiplicity of ideals and forces, and there is always a surplus, as outlined in Chapter One, regarding the nature of the Freudian Molecule.

Martin Luther King Jr's dream can be misunderstood as an ideal of a "post-racist" society, in that the speech itself can be recognized as simply this abstract concept of post-racism, or the impossible idea of a power which rules over all of mankind to overcome racism. It is more accurately known by the now popular phrase "anti-racist," which is a force that may include the racial prioritizing of the needs of one race over the other, in order to act in a manner which pays fidelity to the idea of race being linked with oppressive power, rather than a mere abstract antagonism to a race. This is not to speak of this as the right way to see things over the dialectical material model, but rather a demonstration of an idea which sees itself articulated in force in the world, both in institutions and in spoken word.

Racism is not something to be overcome, but is itself the process of overcoming. Paraphrasing Farrakhan, the holocaust memorial is not forgotten, and neither is slavery. This, however, misses the first fundamental principle of rational self-interest in that Martin Luther King Jr's speech was itself a molecule which existed in actuality at a certain point in history, and was thus actual force toward the idea of anti-racism, articulating in the (supposed) elimination of segregation laws. This molecule is historically remembered in a way that tearing down statues will not be, which is not to discount the historical importance of the dental-like removal of statues which signify racism through the lack of the acknowledgment of racism due to a past molecular fantasy of the great man. Martin Luther King Jr has an embodiment of expertise that others do not.

Society appears to constantly be on the lookout for the next great molecule. Some look toward the Hong Kong protesters as a sign of the ideal of free speech appearing within communist society, a fantasy of the final barrier to overcome the notion that capitalism offers something extraordinarily important that a communist society does not: free speech. Once again, this is in the form of an ideal, and while there is force in that direction, it is not enough force to actualize it.

The quantity of protesters, just as the quantity of statue downers, quality in the form of a subject-supposed-to-know, suggest that there is no central point of control which will suddenly enact a large societal change. But it is not as simple as that, for the quality of Martin Luther King Jr's existence rested in part on the possibility and quantity of people who demanded anti-racist change, and specifically an end to segregation

The anti-racist ideal is different than the "I Have A Dream" speech in that the ideal contains a timelessness, but the speech itself was delivered on August 28, 1963. Dr King's speech, "In a sense we've come to our nation's capital to cash a check. When the architects of our republic wrote the magnificent words of the Constitution and the Declaration of Independence (Yeah), they were signing a promissory note to which every American was to fall heir."[12]

The importance of mastery in The Good Cause, to center the speech around a person who is seen as a valid embodiment of the ideal, allows for the force of the ideal to reduce drag, increase efficiency in producing the molecular events which add force to the ideal. When one holds the means of producing an object which is intrinsic to an idea, administrative control immediately becomes a sort of mastery, whether in the form of actual knowledge and expertise which is a rational pursuit or in the form of pure agency, subject-supposed-to-know.

Platforms such as Facebook and Twitter can manufacture this agency through followers, more easily escaping true mastery of the subject. This is not simply a social media phenomenon, as the agency of knowledge is absolutely split with the actual knowledge in its properties, although they have a dialectical relation to each other.

An appeal to an ideal is required for mastery, teleological, and the process can emerge in parts or its entirety retroactively or falsely.

Thus we are thrown to the wind in the hope of finding a true master of something, and the tiers of novice participants, intermediate repeaters, reproducers, or "craftsman," and expert "masters" should be analyzed for their role in mastery. These registers are, like in the Freudian unconscious, transcendent and make a mockery of what they represent constantly, as agency and knowledge are absolutely split, and when they become unified they create a superegoic force, an imposition of that knowledge as valid and its demands as valid as well.

Organizations may act as a buffer to the novice's sophistic ambition toward an idea, such as becoming licensed to do therapy, or becoming a doctor or lawyer, but it is not always clear where one is sourcing the elements which are posited as the idea. Thus, a rational teleology of idealism can assist in determining structural, individual, and other functions of mastery which appear before us, whether or not they appear in order.

The novice chooses, stumbles across, or is otherwise exposed to an idea which is already in the world, and is already mediated by will and demand for an ideal. The novice is fundamentally becoming accustomed to the idea which is already present in the world and mediated through society. This is to say, the idea comes into contact with novices, intermediate craftsmen, and dictators of the idea or "masters," previous to the individual engagement with the idea.

Immediately we are exposed to the problem of sophistry, as all levels of engagers with the idea may posit a mastery when a novice (a true knowledge deficiency), or novice nature from that of a master, such as Socrates and his assertion of non-knowledge. This description assumes that the sophists have been weeded out to some extent and that there is a rational progress toward a mastery, a mastery which ultimately transforms once more into a variety of surplus subjectivities.

The novice comes to know ideas as socially determinate, and knows the idea in its immediate, obvious external reflection. The novice is one who contains primordial self-knowledge, and passes through various stages of engagement with the idea. The novice contains a will toward the idea struck through with fantasy and the negative force of will. The idea is suppositional to the novice, and the novice, while determined to be solidified within the ideal, may be cast out when their engagement with the ideal is seen as rudimentary, and does not pass with ease through the ideal, inhabiting different necessary roles for the singular human being within the ideal. However, at times a single signifier and what can be seen as a non-grasping of the original essential qualities of the idea emerge and a new mastery emerges out of the same signifier, creating a schism. In the Catholic Church, the split between "John Bosco" and "Don Bosco" makes this tendency apparent in the different sects of the same saint, as well as Christianities, many schisms regarding the same Jesus signifier. They inhabit different ideals while appealing to the same man (similar to, most obviously, Christ himself.)

Students find themselves in the role of novice quite often and are in many senses structurally determined novices no matter the level of expertise. Administrators of students demand of them to play a role and engage with a particular idea as a method of training to engage with ideas qua their socially determined value, qua a mastery over the social in general. "Student" is the fundamental novice nature of the idea and the novice, as a buyer of a product spans from the novices, intermediate craftsmen, and dictators of the idea within. The novice is marked by failing self-certainty, and an inability to generate the craft in a manner which could generate the ideal, as determined by the teacher-master/teacher-craftsman.

The craftsman, a teacher who doesn't posit themselves as a generator of an ideal, or someone who cites another and attempts to re-enact that other, the intermediate structural position, engages with the idea to a level in which they have some skill in engaging with the idea in a manner which to experts and novices is deemed a true engagement with the idea. This speaks nothing to their knowledge, which could be more than someone who posits themselves the master of an ideal. The knowledge engagement is what separates the intermediate from the novice; however, due to the necessity of authenticity of turning into its radical opposite in order to further define and once again fail itself, the intermediate idea manufacturer finds himself objectively thinking of himself in a subservient position for a "master," by necessity due to the striking of the self or other as a reproducer in order to achieve true engagement.

Only through the striking of a second object as an inauthentic source can one refine to the level of recreating the ideal, for the intermediate craftsman position.

This finds itself in unity however, in the Martin Luther King example, as he cites the others as master, the framers of the constitution, while discussing how they lack in following through on their ideals, and he points out their ideals as having internal inconsistency. The leader of The Good Cause through this manner elevates himself from craftsman to master of the ideal, and able to create molecular force based on how many people consider him a subject-supposed-to-know, and whose effectiveness has a dialectical relation to the true knowledge of the subject. Knowledge-mastery and agency-master, knowledge and power, come together to create a unity of force, a true leader.

Chapter 11

Leaders of The Good Cause

Mastery is flawed in a way in which power qua power leads the knowledge of the cause to be destroyed by power itself. Power qua power then presupposes itself toward knowledge, power which is to say the ability to generate aspects of the ideal which is not yet ideal, but is in-and-for itself power more than ideal.

This power qua power determinacy is checked by a social determinacy of the master as master of an ideal, a leader of The Good Cause. In generating this social determinacy and the expanding of one's own ideas, craft now becomes registered as the idea, insofar as it is desired to be part of the craft by novices, craftsmen, and masters who are also engaged with the ideal. The status of the academic who just tried to repeat the idea previously or those who act as a vessel are freed from the idea of having to carry within one's own failing subjectivity an intrinsic power which carries the ideal to determine new lines of the idea immediately.

Socialism must enter the framework here, and we have to consider that administrative control, as well as material wealth, can allow one to generate validity within the social registers to a certain extent. One can create material apparatuses which work toward the ideal, and thus a Mastery, a power-knowledge, is able to be formed with little force opposing the legitimacy of the claim due to the power of the claimant.

Power then reveals itself as a source of valid knowledge which can destroy the rationality of the knowledge itself during determinate moments of time. It can create force which is antithetical to an ideal, force which is only possible through power posting itself as knowledge

When the academic master can generate the idea through

retroactive posit, which is positing something which was there which was not posited prior, the material or administrative backing ultimately has no total check on the validity of the cause. The cause in this way has no ground but the ground of self-interest in the world. The word or demand of master who is in fact master qua material or administrative control can then go into law and the history of the idea.

This is, however, once more negated when one reminds one's self of the transcendental character of idea as well as mastery itself, and novices may throw facts and random information out which then get integrated into the psychic wills of others and then articulated as demands by masters, or those positing themselves as masters, but a quantity of masters of the ideal, ideal which is outside of control of a single master, can return as the repressed content of the obscured ideal.

Once a leader does this, he is revealed to not be a simple dictator of the ideal. The collision of masters and powers jockey with each other to determine validity, and thus the ideal in the world, held together by signifiers and signs, emerges to challenge any would-be total re-writer of history. When novices challenge the dictator, they are challenging both the direction of the ideal and the master's self-certainty as master, which is to say, the master's ability to generate the ideal through his statements.

A leader of a good cause is necessarily challenged in order to preserve the fidelity of the ideal in the world, but if a leader has material and administrative mastery which can create mandates backed by administrative force through law, violence, and monetary backing, it may be difficult to challenge such a leader, as Trotsky may have come to understand in his challenges of Stalin through the realm of antithetical speech.

Conflict is the necessity of fidelity of an ideal as mandated by a master.

The master assumes leadership, but is always a master

who contains within himself a superego imposition of his own legitimacy, and comes into conflict with those moving ideals, and thus is unified with the master through the ideal engagement.

Chapter 12

Territorial Molecules

Insofar as civilizations crumble, so do territories and their usage for their ideals. Territories in space which have been previously used for the ideal do not necessarily contain the ideal, and thus do not necessarily contain a transcendental being-for-ideal. If the territory is still used by human beings, the territory is still Earth, but not being-for-ideal unless necromancy is done and the territory for the idea is re-asserted.

Actual territory, in so far as it is not for an ideal, nor is it a map of itself through ideal, will nonetheless contain elements which are rationally present, substance outside of ideal. This is not to say this cannot be created through ideal, something built in the name of the ideal, but it can lose the quality of the ideal all together. Territory in-and-for ideal is a separate mediating quality of the actual territory as the container of multiple ideals, mediated through the singular, cybernetic goal. The multiple is in the nature of things brought into existence, and territorial molecules contain a multiplicity of ideals present within the structure.

Insofar as ideal interacts with itself, the ideal takes into account and brings into frame a second ideal, through the actual territory. Remnants of the structure may remain unseen, and return once again, as repressed content.

A being-for-ideal is thus dirempted, insofar as ideal is split through the actual territory outside of the ideal. The quality of the territory which is outside of the ideal determines the function of the territorial molecule within the world.

A question of what is actual territory comes into frame, and here I pose a unity through rationality of virtual territories and material land. While dirempted, they function in a unity regarding self-interest properties and molecules; despite having a few differences of material quality, there is no inside the world and outside the world qua virtuality, but only territories subject to ideals, subject to the force of material production, administration, and mastery of ideals, mastery dirempted by actual knowledge of the ideal and agency.

The content of a second ideal held by a single territory is brought into frame by human agency, and a determination is made as to the relation of this content in the Freudian Molecule which is subject to mediation in the world through the multiplicity of demands, as grounded in the movement of will and demand, and articulation and de-articulation which is the real movement of self-interest through time.

Territory which is in-and-for ideal confronts its particularity in the form of the questioning of it being the territory for an ideal through the ideal's movements of mastery from people firstly, and secondly through the same territory holding a second, rationally known ideal.

People of an ideal can come together and embody a unity, and people then can become a territory of the ideal itself. Being molecular in form, and The Good Cause needed an agent which has validity, interpersonal relationships as well as relationships between rationally known agents come into play. The world becomes apparent as a unity between people and territories, between the material world and virtual spaces, as self-interest articulating itself through The Good Cause, and through interpersonal relations of territories and people, people who reveal themselves to be territories for ideals themselves.

The actual territory outside the ideal is not the ideal, but the ideal which is molecularly embedded in the territory has a unity between the territory and the holders of ideals, in novice-understander, intermediate-repeater, and master-creator forms. Thus the ideal appears from the realm in the form of event, but can be held by territory which is in-and-for the ideal, engaging with its own contractions, as well as the multiplicity of ideals within it and that are related to it.

This takes the form of an interpersonal discourse between ideals and themselves, both rationally outside in the form of an interpersonal discourse, and thus general qualities are ascribed to ideals as well as notions of good or bad, beautiful or not beautiful, useful or not useful, and the force of self-interest in the form of ideal arises to produce force in the articulations of the world, as they enter into discourse with themselves.

What are the two institutions saying to each other? Are they friends? Who has the power in the relationship? These are all interpersonal questions, as well as articulations of self-interest. These are not random, or simply hallucinatory, but they take the form of will which manifests psychologically in an articulated demand as a result of the end of the debate between two ideals, or two people, allies, or enemies. In other words, with a clearer understanding of self-interest, we can track the symptoms and contradictions of ideals throughout history and time.

C: The Communal and Interpersonal

Chapter 13

Agreements, Identity, Order

I. Agreement
II. Identity
III. Order

I. The simplest form of a union is a simple Agreement. This Agreement may be immediately imposed by a territory for an ideal, or previous interactions by others, or it can be an avant-garde creation. Further, we can describe this agreement in human terms as the most animal combination of subjects when inhabited by human subjectivities. A bird picks the parasites off a mammal and the two subjectivities are in a felt agreement, where the will-to-eat and the {will-toward-comfort, will-toward-hygiene, will-toward-sensation} (could we call this set an animalistic drive toward a civilization?) combine in mutual agreement. In humans, the agreement creates a foundation for Civilization, which in agreements feedback *not on themselves i.e.., the content of their sets, but rather on the Agreement itself.* The content of the sets is what is feeding into itself, but the feeding into, or the mechanism of the Hyperstate, which is to say the logical movements of self-interest through time, into the next level is not the content.

Through the expansion of the Agreement form, a demand from the silent desire of the consistency for the demand is created.

II. The provision includes for the first time a secondary leap of agreement, and articulates a desire for consistency, though an identity is created in some sense through the silent agreement, and identity is created when a Provision for an already existing agreement is made. More than agreement upon agreement (like the squirrel hording for the winter in a tree used by a previous generation of squirrels, a previously agreed upon tree). The identity is given as a provision for continual actions within a set of self-interests, an essential component of this advanced, secondary level of agreement, and functions as an agreement about agreement. This agency of identification, in all its failure to describe, can be understood in its form of an agreement about agreement. The identity agrees that further agreements will be handled in a certain way, or if they are not, that they are handled in a way which is against identity. This against-identity may itself be a manifestation of will, in that a will is enjoyed against identity. In the agreement's final form, this takes a cognitive stance of order.

Held together by the identity, in other words, an agency, an identity takes on a quality of an agreement for a consistent set of actions or articulations. An ideal bolstered with an identity for this second order agreement to provide a future sort of guarantee on articulations. Identity and attachment are thus linked, as well as identity and the ability to trust. Identity in a sense is one and the same with trust, and to not be trustworthy can mean the loss of the identity entirely at times.

III. The next categorical stage of identity, which is to say its next categorical movement, is that of Order. This is the turn away from identity or the image as a guarantee, and further defines the identity as a more specific knowing of a guarantee. Avant-garde orders of libertarianism guarantee a set of values which the Libertarian Party does not guarantee. Orders within parties advocate for specific interests. Identity through an order, or subset of that identity, bolsters trust, and guarantees future articulations more strongly in the form of trust.

Chapter 14

Friendships

The friendship is bolstered by identity, or even splits in identity.

Since friendships consist of agreements to interrelate, and agreements do not necessarily have to have more than a felt connection to do a task, self-interest can escape the form of ideal and move into the form of interpersonal friendship

The friend is a simple form of all relations, highly voluntary in most cases, but also friends can be made through territories for ideals, or even through people themselves, as a person's validity becomes its own ideal, surpassing any ideal in the world besides the single individual. To know the stranger and not afford special privileges through feeling makes the friend the most rational of all possible relations in a sense that they are not unified with obligated feelings of a family member, community member, or lover. The friend is split in that it posits two people which may be arbitrary toward a community role in which one serves the community demand, or the family member whom one serves through the demand of the idea of the family.

The friend is positionally different than family in that there is no necessity of a love bond or sex bond within it, as there is in the family. A negative of love and a negative of community or family obligation makes the friend a free-floating relation which offers itself as the most decoded interpersonal interactions.

This fact, however, is negated when we look closer into the friend and find it in places not as decoded as places such as the community relation. A community relation involves one taking up a role within a community and another taking up a role and interacting through these roles. This negation is once more negated when we look at the ground of self-interest as articulated events, and a friendship working on a community project to articulate something, or to mutually participate in an event, can be an extension of friendship or even the beginning of friendship

Insofar as the unity of love and friendship occurs, specifically in the form of a romantic relationship, it may at first appear to be a negation of the friendship, but instead it actually performs the function of articulating a core function of friendship, which is to say an identity agreement.

If sex enters the fray of the friendship, it becomes an order of friendship, either a relationship, or a "friends with benefits" styled situation, where friendship of a particular kind can flourish.

This can be more mundane as well, as friends may come together through a transgression of a particular type of superego imperative in the world. Identity as a "leftist" becomes an order as defined in the beginning of Section C, in that it further articulates in the form of a leftist who doesn't like the superego imperatives of leftism. Or black leftists form an order who don't like the superego imperatives to ignore race which they might come across in other orders of leftism.

Transgression here becomes a basis for friendship. Transgression contains a solid foundation for trust in that it posits not only itself, but an antithesis of a second identity.

Transgression, as well as transgression which transgresses transgression (an order which is against an order; for example, many people are anti-Neoreactionary, but most people don't know what a Neoreactionary is, but this is a transgression against a transgression), can be analyzed as a structure which articulates content in the world.

The long history of the imperative to be healthy along with the effects of reacting against this imperative leads us to a point where the contradiction of health and unhealth merge together within the discussion of what should constitute the ground of being. If the authorities tell me to jog, and my revolutionary comrade tells me the authorities are bad and, in fact, jogging is part of a propaganda campaign to wholesale swallow the validity of what my friends and I have deemed a flawed authority, then what becomes of my relation to jogging?

My relation to jogging becomes mediated by the Big Other, or by the rule set or constellation of ideas in which jogging is determined outside of myself, as well as by my internal fantasies. The movement toward an outside then becomes the question.

Self-interest is the ground of all human existence. It appears within our most private and individualized dreams as well as within the world outside of our conscious knowledge. It appears in our ideas, and the ideas and institutions which are thrust upon us throughout society, as well as the multitude of social dynamics which is the thick molasses of our everyday lives. Everything is covered in it, and it is the reason for the bubbling up of various ideals and things which are representative of ideals.

The Hyperstate, the logic of the actual movement of self-interest, manifests in our choices, and the choices which are made for us without our consultation. The friend is made before the event, and the friend is determined by event, by ghosts of previous articulations.

The friend is casual, and may be linked to power, but it isn't power itself. An ideal of how the world should be, however, is the glass which provides a sort of quantum entanglement of people, linking together their movements.

Self-interest appears most of all as the guiding force which cannot be escaped, that force which pulls the human animal through the thicket of existence. The ideal of how things should be, when agreed upon by two people or two institutions, links them together in the manner that two photons which pass through glass are inexplicitly linked together.

Conscious friendship is not the only way that people are linked together. They are also linked together by the view of how things are, as well as how things should be. Articulations make self-interest maintain its secret in that it morphs into an unrecognizable multiplicity of both harmonious and conflicting pulses of reality within specific moments of time, as well as in the ideas of the times, and of time's collapse back into existence and ideal, and the singularity of power. Control to shape the world becomes in conflict and harmony with the ideas of the world itself, and is split in two when it appears in the will of a single human, and the single human is shown to be unequivocally doomed to their desire from ideological forces which invisibly guide them.

The ways in which people are linked together are unconscious articulations of the symbolic order, of the articulated demands. There is always excess, surplus, and we find ourselves linked together in ways which we did not bargain for.

Chapter 15

Earth Mastery

The subjectivity of the thing which is outside of the individual consciousness (even when it is both inside and outside of the individual consciousness) is not simply ideal insofar as it is unreal, or a concept of the thing, but rather it is known rationally through various properties which it contains. Empirical data is a common accepted scientific standard to know the Earth, how hot the Earth is today in a certain region, and so on.

The signifier of Earth is important in that it groups together the world as a whole, and thus the idea of the mastery over it haunts mankind, and will continue to haunt mankind. Ideas of the wholeness of the Earth manifest in ideas of a global control system, and this global control system idea demonstrates to us its radical opposite, which is that there is no single point of control over the Earth.

God covers the dream of the single point of control of Earth, and through single points of control we can know the essence of the God idea. For the New-Ager, God is the universe, yes, but insofar as the universe then becomes in Idea a single point. For the monotheists, God becomes the single point of reason, the single point of wisdom, the single point of justice, and so on.

God is in essence the dream of the Mastery over Earth, and all which that can contain. Kings become vessels for God, the King being unable to manage the idea of a lack of control, since their power in their domain must for them dwarf all others who dare to have control within that domain. The King dares not to posit themselves as the end in all, for that is a fatal weakness. If the King is the Absolute End, the Idea to kill the King becomes all too immediate. God is the negative of Power through greater Power, but a greater Power which does not actually exist in a single point of control, if we are to be atheists here.

The existentialist notion that God remains in the world through properties of God makes some sense, but it is not brutal enough. God's main property is the single point of control. In polytheistic cultures, gods take on a single point of control for various ideas, and in the case of Zeus the idea of a god then gets taken under control as well.

In the Ender's Game Series, the dream of Earth coming into a single point of rational control through the Hegemon is taken up with religious fervor by Orson Scott Card through various texts. Orson Scott Card details the many flaws of the man who does eventually become hegemon of Earth, as well as detailing how that lofty title fails. The fantasy, however, consists in the hegemon gaining not just more and more power, but more and more rational control over himself and the world around him.

The environmentalist in the abstract has a different dream, which is to say the unhuman dream of the Earth taking control of itself. This is not to say there is not a role which humanity needs to play, but that role is often the negation of humanity itself. Humanity's impact is known as a Power, and the Earth Master is the Master which takes from the Earth its in and of itselfness. This is negated by theories such as we are the environment, and the collapsing of the bifurcation of man and nature, and into the single unit which is Earth mastering itself.

The Earth as the single ontological object can be known to master itself, and thus the history of those who have tried to center any sort of Earth Mastery within themselves is a caravan of foolishness and caution. Dreams of world domination are classic tales of Earth Mastery gone wrong, but that is only the realm of the political, the rule of man.

The creative amateur seems to be no master, and seems to know nothing. But the dream of the master is alive in the creative amateur, who dares not call himself master. He is, however, firmly within the idea of mastery. The master like

God knows all. But God is a human creation, something which signals its radical opposite. The ideal of mastery fails when power is understood as a process. Power, as it is held in its human form, moves strangely just as the ground of humanity does. The human thing is the self-interested thing which escapes the signifier of both self and interest but is nonetheless both in process.

Despite the dream of Earth Mastery being an abject failure, there can be the goal which links people together, which entangles people within an identity, causing them to spin and articulate in service of it, for better or worse.

Chapter 16

The Beautiful

The beauty which is woman, or which is fish, or which is the felt feeling of ecstasy, or which is present in art, or that which is laminated and printed for 25 cents and stuck on the side of a tent on the street all have in common the signifier, the linguistic thing of beauty. There are, of course, more shades of beauty than the beauty signifier, for one thing this is in the English language which has its own linkages to beauty.

An antithetical picture to beauty is man who fucks. What is more absurd than the man who fucks? He can never be, he must control beauty, but he is forever outside of it. The woman becomes the man who fucks, the man becomes the woman, but we can know this as the man who fucks and we know the thing which grasps at beauty. Certainly, there is some sort of unity possible between identifying one's self as beautiful while fucking, a homoerotic identification of the self as erotic.

To grasp at beauty is always to be covetous of beauty and the power of beauty to be beauty. If one cannot do, one must teach? If one cannot be, one must have! But if one has it and is not it, how much does one have exactly? Beauty becomes out of reach of the commoner who has it all, and becomes immediately at hand for those who have nothing.

A certain humbleness must come in order to appreciate beauty, a willingness to see something outside one's self as beautiful, temporarily putting the self on the backburner. Is it not plain to see that those who are narcissistic, gazing always at the self, fail to see beauty in the world?

Beauty has escaped those who attempt to grasp it, especially when one grasps it. The beautiful, those who are beautiful in some respect, become misers of what they once were, and become something else entirely. So in order to escape this trap, we come to know beauty. The thing which knows beauty has let go of the idea of the single point of control, and in that letting go is able to see what truly is. One must let go of the single point of control in order to see what is because if one looks for a single point of control, they only see what they control or delude themselves into thinking that they have a control which they do not. So then one becomes one who knows beauty.

To create an ideal then, one can interject the thing which is beautiful. One sacrifices the object of the self, in order to unite the object of the ideal with the object of beauty.

When there is an interest in the beautiful, then one pulls one's self out of immiseration. There is a pseudomasochism in knowing the beauty, in its split from being the beauty to a certain extent, but there can be a recognition of one's self to some extent in the beauty, making beauty in-and-for-itself as it is for the other, for the person gazing upon it. This can be as simple as being the identity of someone who knows the beautiful.

The self can make itself the ideal and beauty actual, as well. It paints on itself, its will, its world. It sees beauty with its eyes, and hears beauty in the music. The actual beauty becomes in the end something which moves through the world wildly, jumping registers and ideas, as all things which are linguistically present do.

The creative becomes one who creates beauty, as limited as that beauty may be. By seeing the beauty the person creates beauty, but by seeing, hearing, making, and knowing the beauty in its multiplicity one gains what looks to the amateur like a mastery of the thing, a single point of control, but is in fact something which has finally become in line to the reality of the thing, the process of the thing which is beauty in its multitude.

The dream of the single point of control goes back into the Will, but the Will is known as this small thing which one has, something which is not that necessary to get bent out of shape about. Something which can, if we are lucky enough, produce something beautiful.

Chapter 17

Order Contra Identity

Men fighting for their own liberty and prestige are very different creatures from men who are called upon to use their judgement, unclouded by passion, when the fight is over.
Titus Livus[13]

I would sell my mother into slavery to see a V for Vendetta Part 2.
Slavoj Zizek[14]

The identity, being vague and open, something with potential, is beaten back by order, by a demand for specificity. But the demand for specificity flips itself, and reduces the appearance of its own demand, it covers itself with identity. Identity being both a positive and negative possibility, the negative of identity pulls the force of the positive identity through articulations which are representative of self-interest actualized. There may be absolute antagonism between positive and negative identities in principle. The negative identities are absolutely true, but primordial, unformed, and process-based, while positive identities are demands articulated. Both contain force, but the positive identity is prone to the psychoanalytic forces of the negative. In turn, the negative identities are influences and given structure by the positive, the negative identity becoming exact with will, and the positive becoming exact with demand. Self-interest being temporal, something which appears as a result of their interactions.

The Ego Substance contains identity, and identity contains a promissory note, a guide for current and future action. Not only this, it affects past action in the name of the identity, and psychoanalytically creates the return of the past in a form which is actually new, and transcendental in time, immediately at hand with force. The positive order forces the identity into a specific mode of acting. The identity as a person of the high culture or separate from the high culture is not just identity, but a guide or promise toward certain action. This, however, through modernity, is becoming more noticeable as identity becomes something which is more fluid, and less and less of a promise toward certain actions.

The identity becomes secondary to the material wealth of someone to put forth an idea. Here, the myth of identity becomes something which obscures the true relation of power, which is material. An identity can be taken up and discarded, while the process of the identity may be its radical opposite. In *Gladiator*, as discussed earlier, the general had the identity of a farmer, but he nonetheless was functional as a general, not a farmer. Although there was a true desire to be a farmer, he could not escape the process of his own molecular existence as something outside of identity.

The desires and demands of humanity are determined and funneled, understood through language and ideas, and as an exploration of what rational self-interest entails, but we must look at the self-contradictory nature of the individual subject to understand the nature of self-interest.

True rational identity can appear as a negative, an identity which can be rationally known but is disavowed. A person can be an idiot, and if they disavow this and posit themselves as a genius, insofar as they are actually an idiot, this negative identity will continue to pull them in a set of actions. In fact, this negative identity has more force, because it is one with the Hyperstate, and its logical existence is absolutely correct. A posited identity will always be weaker than a negative, hidden identity, which is aligned absolutely with the true processes of the person.

The negative pulls in order to resolve conflict and reveal the rational movement of The Ego Substance. Reason does march through the world, but it has a cloak on.

The Ego Substance is made up of positive and negative identity, with negative identity being the more powerful. Since the positive identity makes a promise in the form of an articulated identification of the self, one falls short. The unarticulated identity, however, pulls like gravity toward processes.

The ruling class marches on through the negative. The idiot who gains power through nepotism or otherwise asserts the positive identity of genius, but the negative identity of family sameness may pull them through.

Myth obscures self-interest into ideologies, the Hyperstate reveals the negative identity and makes it positive, thus revealing the orders of mankind. The Freudian Molecule is seen in dreams, where things combine to create objects, and the dialectic engagement flushes out contradictions and logically analyzes the interactions between categories and objects. This is not to say people are simply a set of tendencies within negative space, but the acknowledgment of The Ego Substance and its movements known as the Hyperstate is a revealing of the negative. Once the symptom is identified, once the true power is known, adjustments can be made. Power can be encountered.

D: Pure Unconscious Rational Force

Chapter 18

Absolute Particularity

*The moral standpoint is the standpoint of the will, not in its abstract or implicit existence, but in its existence for itself, an existence which is infinite. **This turning back of the will upon itself**, or its actual self-identity, with its associated phases stands in contrast to its abstract implicit existence, and **converts person into subject...***

...the will of the subject, though it still retains traces of self-involved simplicity, is the will of an individual, who is an object for himself. Hence **subjectivity is the realization of the conception — This gives freedom from a higher ground.** GWF Hegel[15]

Hegel, failing to know will as the negative force of the unconscious, includes this statement in *The Philosophy of Right* in the section on morality. This leads to a dialectical sublation of the will into Purpose and Responsibility, Good and Conscious, then into An Ethical Life. Clearly, Hegel is not working from the notion of egoism, psychological or ethical; the understanding of the will as pure conscious intention, with no real analysis of what lies beneath the surface of rationality. The psychoanalytic impulses of humanity, ultimately articulating through society and the world as demands which are rationally understood. Then Hegel presupposes an alignment with these notions of the conscious mind. This is due to a superego imperative to inscribe into consciousness all of society, and align one's self to it to some extent, and to denigrate the individual actor and notions contra that society articulated in the state. The issue here is that the power of the state is not the force to end all forces, because the material force of ideas are in contradiction with each other. In other words, Hegel in *The Philosophy of Right* is, famously, not Hegelian enough.

Hegel articulates the following in favor of conscious unity with the state:

> The state is rational in and for itself in as much as it is the actuality of the substantial will which it possesses in the particular self-consciousness that has been raised to its universality. This substantial unity is an absolute unmoved end in itself, in which freedom comes into its supreme right. On the other hand, this final end has supreme right against the individual, whose supreme duty is to be a member of the state. If the state is confused with civil society, and if its specific end is laid down as the security and protection of property and personal freedom, then *the interest of individuals as such* becomes the ultimate end of their association, and it follows that membership of the state is something optional. But the state's relation to the individual is quite different from this. Since the state is objective spirit, it is only as one of its members that the individual himself has objectivity, truth, and ethical life. Unification as such is itself the true content and aim, and the individual's destiny is to live a universal life.[16]

What Hegel is suggesting here is fairly off the map in terms of contemporary relationships with the state. Here perhaps the conscious alignment of the laws would produce a unity of consciousness with universality.

What Hegel is truly suggesting here is an identity. A promise of future action in service of the state, as well as a guide for action which is united with the movements of Absolute Spirit.

If Hegel had done this, would it not be in service of his own self-interest, including acting against himself, for his own ideal? Ideal takes the form of identity, and becomes articulated in moments. Hegel could certainly have a grand time acting against the wishes of other humans in the name of the state, and that would have been in his self-interest via his identity as a patriot.

The simple socialist reminder here is that we are not all Hegel. For the one who serves the state is not necessarily rewarded in kind. Explicitly, Hegel states that the state acts against individual wishes and agreements with each other. Certainly Hegel was able to find favor within his identity of a man of the state, but this is not always the case. For him, this unity of movement may have been an end in itself, but this is an order, a manifestation of a particular identity.

The reduction of possibility to the ethical function of the state reduces the possibility of universal rationality itself. In the hope to unify one with the ethical spirit of the state, via Right, one reduces all of mankind to litigators. What sort of artist would one be who limited themselves to the ethical articulations of state identity? Certainly this would be a type of artist, but this artist could not produce anything that was united with a universal spirit against the state which they inhabit, for instance.

The limiting of identity to that of the state is in fact not in and for itself as Hegel claims, as it reduces the ability to engage with what is other, except as antithetical to rationality. Freud's truth can be summed up in part as the limits of rationality. Further expanded, there is in fact a rationality to irrationality, and in dreams items appear from the unconscious to articulate wishes and anxieties, to truly work through antagonisms. Antagonism purely in the realm of directing thought or morality toward the state is certainly an identity and an order, but it is not in line with what could be said to be the true universal, which is self-interest.

The kingdom of ends forbids the question of self-interest, and it is easy to see why! It is the logical universal, which must be dismissed off hand if one is to present a non-universal end as an end, a particular identity as a universal identity. This, however, misses the true universal identity, which is the particularity of will and demands to formulate demands in the world in the form of words, materials, movements, and systems meant to be the extension of demand. Articulations which are the result of the true universal unity, self-interest, and the creation of humans which are previous articulations.

The alignment to an articulation of one who was previous without examining the relationship to the self, and to off hand create a vulgar abstraction as a thing to align with is an end in itself, but it is not a universal end.

Chapter 19

The Unconscious Extension of Words and Ideals Via Their Processes

Peace contains within an antithetical notion to the vulgar, non-examined notion of self-interest, which is self-interest absolutely contra the other. As outlined before, it is only antithetical in a superficial form.

Peace is not only peace, but it contains within its ideal a universal supergoic imperative to a regulation of a system toward which antagonisms are reduced to some degree. This can be posited, through various identities and orders, as the opposite of the vulgar notion of peace which is an image rather than peace's logical extension. In other words, "war is peace."

This is not a universal, but a self-interested identity to which "war is peace" can truly be toward a reducing of antagonisms within a system. Certainly the nation believes war is peace to some extent, and alignment with one's nation would mean alignment with its wars. If that nation also valued peace within its constitution, then peace would be war by Hegel's system.

An idea like peace could be incorporated into The Ego Substance through its articulation which besides via order, agreement, and identity, can be done within one's own consciousness and movements within the world. Articulations of that peace come through in molecular form. Which is to say, even if that peace were through the identity of the state, the state identity would create articulations which were extended past the state, containing the negative force of will.

To ignore the negative force of will allows all sorts of things to run parallel to the state. In America, racist idealism runs quite easily parallel to the state through the state's right. One can become a police officer, and in unity with the process of law, enforce the law in areas which have been determined to be areas which require heavy policing, carrying over from racist segregations of the past. Racism went from standard policy to terrorist status in less than a century. Although racism is counter to the official values of the state, it can run in unity with the state identity quite easily via ideological obfuscation, as evidenced by Trumpism.

An identity or a subset of identity in the form of the more particular order contains the possibility for the conditions of will to be enacted through a positive demand which bears no resemblance to the will. In other words, the ethics of Hegel have been self-defeating as it eliminates the condition for its own major posit, which is its own universality, continuing Kant's immediate dismissal of self-interest, undoubtedly due to an aesthetic aversion to the word.

Peace which knows itself can be said to be of an identity of peace, which can further be given the articulations of itself in the world, through determinate moments, to determine that the peaceful subject creates further grounds for its own demand to be enacted.

Peace here faces a problem, however. The peaceful subject always fails in becoming an Absolute peaceful subject, in terms of the ideal of peace as a lack of antagonism, due to the necessity that it must change what is around in order to be peaceful.

Within the ideal of peace, then, is its own absolute antithesis, destruction. This can be easily glanced over if one refuses the notion of Absolute Particularity, but the event within time, the particular growth of a particular rose rather than the universal rose which is a seed, then stem, then blooming flower, then wilting stalk, to be known as truly what it is. The particular self-interest which contains a unity of the ideal of self-interest, but articulates in different manners. The destruction of what is, destruction being rationally identifiable, is within the notion of peace. Peace being a unity of antagonisms, what is unpeaceful, thus contains superego in the form of unity. The destroying subject and the peaceful subject are united as The Ego Substance, however, and its nature as self-interest is never lost, despite claims to anti-particularity in the form of universalist unity. The specter of the destroying subject can be said to haunt the self-interest of the peaceful subject.

One can argue that The Ego Substance deviates from self-interest in the process of self-interest articulated directly as a peace identity containing destructive will, but this charge would be of the image of self-interest rather than the knowledge of self-interest as The Ego Substance's movement through time. A duty ethic which considers laws and citizens and other such specters is ultimately an identity, positing force against the other except as an extension of its own identity.

Both the Hegelian subject and the Kantian subject can be said to be followers of the maxim of peace, which finds an ends in a unity of consciousness with something in the world, or something transcendentally ethical. This is only a unity with an identity, and thus is limited in its ability to explain the true content of the world context of a particular nation, even with the inevitability of war.

A peaceful subject is not entirely separate from an explicitly destructive subject, both being idyllic and determined through identity, identity which can be forced from material conditions. Both can function to kill, and both can function to create articulations which contain the actual movement of wish extension in the world. This is how a horror of identity is possible, the unity of opposite imperatives due to identity being an agreement.

The subject articulating for one aim contains the negative will of its opposite, rationally identifiable. Thus the articulation becomes the form in which self-interest can be said to lie absolutely, rather than in the ideals themselves. The articulations in the world are grounded in self-interest, the resolutions of demand and will through what is actual, which nonetheless never offers a pure kingdom of ends, never a single end in itself, but rather an absolute substance regarding its movements.

Chapter 20

The Unity of Differentiating Forces Through Articulations

Wills which are primordial and not yet articulate, or not yet mined, the result of an ideological gap or surplus within an articulation, as well the goal or demand itself, attempt to find an equilibrium through logic. What is more, at times they work together, they work against each other, and work independently of each other in the service of a logical synthesis. But this is not the true nature of their unity. The unity of opposites occurs within moments of articulation.

Wills which work with demand toward differing ideals may work with each other to form a singular articulation in the world. A Democrat and Republican, for instance, both work together to articulate an election. While the representative may be of either party, the election itself is a unity of supposed opposites, not to comment on the true "oppsitional" nature of the two major United States parties.

The superego here will flare up to deny there is true unity, but unity in time there is. The calls for unity of the nation in an electoral system will undoubtedly be very popular in the assertion of things which both ideals must do to perpetuate themselves. This process is self-interest in the world, elections are self-interest in the form of identities coming together, in opposition, through various articulations.

Wills, unconscious in the form of desires as well as logical negative identities, which appear to work toward the same desire working against each other in self-interest, create unitary expressions articulated in the world. To say any state, which is an articulation of these identities and self-interests in the unity of say, an event of a war, and a winning of a particular ideal, contains a universal duty as Hegel describes in *The Philosophy of Right*, would be painting over the nature of these states as articulations of the true universal, which is self-interest, articulated in unitary events, actions, battles, conflicts, and organizations, designed to express self-interest as well as to assert ideals over other ideals. Caleb Majeski, anarchist astrologist and novice poker player, suggested to me that "the lack of unity necessitates reasons."

Insofar as there is a contradiction, we can see that the contradiction is limited in its scope in accessing the consequences of the event as the universal, but the event itself is a unity, and the event which is a unity of oppositional forces contains within it the multiplicity of forces articulated as self-interest, as well as the surplus of those forces in the Freudian Molecular form. Which is not to forget the first chapter, where the synthetic nature of the articulation in the world creates a surplus which exceeds a simple, single logic.

The history of psychology and various psychoanalyzes or psychotherapies have attempted to grasp at these contradictions in various manners, but the whole has never been grasped. Cognitive dissonance is present in the unity of event, and action which appears peaceful may be destructive, and action which appears destructive is the enacting of self-interest in the world. Vulgar notions of peace, including peace-of-mind, do not understand that self-interest is a time traveler when it contains the wishes of a past event to resolve in a different way, hopping desires, particular acts, and ideals which are present in the world outside of itself.

Ideal is actual in the world, fighting other ideals, fighting that which is not ideal when it is united in the world through material. Fighting itself insofar as its own logic, the ideal in its conflicts internal and external is self-interest articulating itself through time.

The exact logic of this is the concept of The Ego's Hyperstate.

The end result of the movement of ideas is in fact the means to desire to articulate. This wish is accessed partially, through the extension of the ideals past their abstraction, and into their concrete articulations.

Chapter 21

The Absolute Hyperstate

The Absolute Hyperstate's self-interest in the world in total is structured somewhat like a dream. This means it can be direct, logical in itself, or form molecular parts in the form of dream content, which is to say a phantasy-based item which is not necessarily revealed in its containment of The Ego Substance. Through identity and order, we begin to see rationality appear, and a consistency of what it posits itself.

But The Absolute Hyperstate is not this narrative which the world reveals to itself, simply self-confirming in its idealism. The vectors of The Ego Substance, through identity, through narrative myth, and all the other articulations and de-articulations through time described throughout this study, create a world which is laid on top of the entire world. The entire world justifies itself with its positive logics, but there is a world which is the process of that world.

There is the state of things, as one takes things as they are, then there is the process of things, and the process of things articulated by humans is to know humans as beings of self-interest.

The Hyperstate is the totality of human existence which can be accessed past the initial given logics. The articulations and de-articulations reveal themselves to be modes of self-interest. So long as the explanation of an event denies the existence of self-interest, well, we can see that this is the normal state of things. The normal state of things pushes out knowledge of the movements of its interest.

The ideal carries with it The Ego Substance, or a property of self-interest in the form of the power of the ideal. It can reveal itself to be a true ideal which is both reflected to itself as consistent, and a good universal rule. This is, of course, the state of things. The state justifies itself with itself, and this is the state of things. The true articulations of the state through its institutions and actors, as representing the logical actualities of the events which have occurred, and the ideals which transcendentally move to assert themselves via not only individual actors, but institutions which presuppose a clash of ideals, this is a part of The Absolute Hyperstate.

A psychological test sorts people into categories of introversion or extraversion, but it is united in the test as structure, and the test taking as event, and the test itself as worth taking. The taking of a test is a working out of two ideals. Diametrically opposite or valid within themselves they are or are not, they perpetuate themselves through history.

This historically falls in the line of psychology tests being invented in the first place, and then the popularization. The articulations of the past create the self-interest of the present. The dreams of the future return to redefine the identities and orders of the past. This is The Absolute Hyperstate. To say it is just a psych test, well, that is certainly the state of things. The first order of knowledge. The ideal itself which is terrified to know it in its own will, its own reason for being.

Max Stirner stated as the title to the introduction of his magnum opus *The Ego And His Own*, "All Things Are Nothing To me!"[17] In this pursuit of the force which drives human history, this can be read as a statement of disgust at the clear split between ideal and The Absolute Hyperstate, or the true logic of the true driving force of being.

In order to counter this, Stirner dreams of not being taken up by the ideal itself, to not be subject to ideology. He would not be fooled by the supposed state of things! The bodily pursuit, and the ideal of self-interest which de-articulates easily when it determines it is not of itself, of self-interest, is ultimately a confession to show that this is not in fact the true nature of self-interest.

Thought is scorned, but thought is what the self is interested in, and is an element of the substance of Ego, of what is unique within an individual, as well as what is the true constitution of the world around us.

To get to the back of things is to understand self-interest in its compositional components, its articulations of event, its pull of what is unseen, and its transformation into ideals. Ideals which contain within them commands to do or not do, ideals which contain superego imperatives. But the superego imperative to enjoy is itself an ideal, and not an escape from superego imperatives as such, which are created in the unity of actual existence, and apparent in the unity of our dreams, where objects, seemingly out of nowhere, come forward to pronounce their existence.

Just as in our dreams, objects, seemingly out of nowhere, but really extensions of the physical world and The Absolute Hyperstate, appear to us to manifest in some form, self-interest. Under the cloak of fiction, of myth, or logic itself, we are presented with pure idealism. With fantasy. But this fantasy is not simply unreal, for in its articulation we bear witness to The Absolute Hyperstate, which is to say we bear witness to the rational articulation of reality.

Afterwards: The Good Place

*The state is rational in and for itself inasmuch as it is the actuality of the substantial will which it possesses in the particular self-conscious that has been raised to its universality. This substantial unity is an absolute end in itself, in which freedom comes into its supreme right. On the other hand, this final end has supreme right **against the individual,** whose supreme duty is to be a member of the state.*
GWF Hegel[18]

Why should one have a supreme duty to be a member of a state? It's a matter of survival and desire certainly. If one lives within a monarchy, or if one lives within a state which has a grip on ideology, duty to the state inevitably becomes a matter of having a venue for one's desire to effectively transfer into one's demands, as well as a matter of survival.

An unconscious power play is strung through Hegel, clear as day, the need to overcome the government with the assertion of the individual. What is supposedly a unity of man and the state, is actually Hegel clinging onto the state for not only survival, but to articulate his own desires, his own will-to-power which manifests in what he wants for himself. In other words, to be the philosopher that he was. But because of this, he couldn't really let the state get one over on him through all moments of the dialectic. The state is also overcome:

...For to us religion means the retirement of the Spirit within itself, in contemplating its essential nature, its inmost Being. In these spheres, then man is withdrawn from his relation to the State, and betaking himself to this retirement is able to release himself from the power of secular government.
Hegel, Philosophy of History (p. 130)

Could Hegel free himself from the bonds of the state without risking life and limb? Yes he could quite easily, and at no risk to manifesting his desires through the identity of the state. Thanks to God, he is able to rest. Is this not a clear unconscious wish to escape the superego of the state, which he has raised to the level of supreme duty?

To state the obvious, Hegel does not escape self-interest, he is in the midst of psychological egoism. His morals and values swirl together with their consequences to create a narrative of absolute duty to the state. (I bet the King loves that!) Hegel does not know why he does what he does, but he certainly has a nice rational system for it. He is determined by unconscious psychological forces

On that note, how great is it that *The Good Place* existed as a show? An articulation of philosophy as a television product with a relatively engaging story line is certainly in line with what I consider an ideal or two, manifesting in the world. A main character is a Kantian in constant moral crisis (and some say that we aren't progressing as a species). Chidi is a philosophical fantasy, the man devoted to the raw calculation of his actions in a totally selfless religious devotion.

How does the Kantian Chidi judge his life? He laments on not doing "enough," like his love interest Eleanor. It seems clear that Chidi has a point; I doubt anyone watched the show and thought Chidi was someone who shouldn't be drawn into the orbit of the Arizonan Egotist Eleanor. Eleanor was defined by the most vulgar ideal of self-interest, which is self-interest contra the well-being of others. She never missed a chance to insult or scam someone.

Her character eventually escaped the negative judgment of itself through consulting with Chidi, the calculative Kantian. But she judged herself negatively for taking the actions of scamming, and by the end of the show she finds love and a sense of self-worth. It is clear with a small amount of rational analysis that she in fact is more self-interested than ever. Chidi moves away from calculation toward the emotive registers and articulations which are at times in line with duty, but at other times are in line with the articulation of desire.

Self-interest mutates, slides, combines, burns, grows, and becomes unrecognizable. Self-interest is the bastard of all ethical theories insofar as it is pegged into a single register, usually the register of "the itch" or the hedonistic, immediate gratification impulse, or the register of its use against other people. Self-interest is indeed both of these things at times. However, self-interest in process is the ground of all ideals and their movements, when overlooked by the holder of the ideal.

In the final calculation, self-interest is revealed through a "that's it!" feeling, a uniting of the characters in ideals, in goals, and in actions. It is a rational expression of survival and desire which make their way through ideals to create particular events, which create forces in their lives, which cause ideals to work themselves out through unitary events and their mutual superego forces.

I am not saying that Chidi should not be a Kantian. In his state of things, he is quite an interesting character. Those of us who are aware of The Absolute Hyperstate shouldn't necessarily be bringing it into every conversational discussion. Rather, The Absolute Hyperstate, the true movement of self-interest, can be utilized to troubleshoot movements through the worlds when necessary. To know that if you encounter Chidi in the wild, that he is in unity with an antagonistic ideal, and that this is self-interest. To articulate that his entire moral framework is incorrect due to not understanding that self-interest is the ground of being, to be insistent on this fact might harm the beauty of the world.

This is a call for you to be an artist to some extent, to be able to see beauty, and know how to intervene in ideals. It is also a call to not let the superego unities overwhelm you, to not feel that there is no escape from any one ideal.

The Vector of Vulgarity

The vulgar does not just consist of the overtly sexual, violent, or dirty, but rather it consists of the rejection of the efforts of a particular civilization. The demand of civilization is a demand of self-interest.

In *The Good Place*, Chidi is clearly civilized, and Ellen is not. But neither have truly acclimated to their environment, which is hell masquerading as heaven. To simply assert Chidi's notions of what is good or civilized proves itself not to be enough, and the egotism of Ellen, self-interest which is the vulgar notion of self-interest contra the other, creates the framework which allows the unity of supposed opposites to create a union which functions for the both of them. This union of self-interest, with those who consider themselves more civilized than the other, occurs with much self-congratulations on the part of the "civilized," who don't take into account the self-interest quality of their efforts, as they articulate their ideals on the other. There is, of course, a mutual working through of ideals.

The vulgar comes into frame in contradiction to what is supposedly civilized. To assert an ideal of civilization must be done to a certain extent through vulgarity, which is to say the actual antagonistic forces of that order in the world.

Ellen was Chidi's vulgarity, and the both of them fell in love, of course. He taught her to get out of his head supposedly, and she was taught to be more idealistic. They were both, of course, adjusting to the system they were in, working out the contradictions of their ideals and their ties to each other episode by episode, articulation by articulation. What needed to be de-articulated: Chidi's stiffness which manifests in indecisiveness, which is a somewhat loveable virture, rendering the male too virtuous, too unperverted! In Lacanian terms, a clear fantasy of the father who does not succumb to desire, who does not have sex. The non-pere-version of the symbolic order of Kant! This fits well with the contemporary meme of Kant being the "volcel," voluntarily celibate philosopher.

The power in vulgarity is two-fold. Firstly, the pushing back of what is determinate and solid in civilization back into the primordial unconscious will, in a way which attempts to challenge the institution. Secondly, the vulgarity has the power to further legitimize power, by giving it more of a character of completeness. Power and its antagonism fight themselves fully in the domain of those who hold power, and the illusion of a revolutionary force appears which is just a puppet of power. This doesn't mean vulgarity doesn't have revolutionary power.

Was it not vulgar of Rosa Parks to sit at the front of the bus? For Marx, the vulgarity of positing class struggle as the basis of history over the ideals of the ruling class.

Jesus Christ appears as a Roman Vulgarity.

When searching for rationality itself in relation to being, one looks at the articulation and the denaturing of what exists. Through the process of a vulgarity which is the breaking through of the current order of things, one can see ideals, the true movements of which are self-interest being played out.

Is it not beautiful?

Are you not entertained?

Endnotes

1 S. Freud, *The Interpretation of Dreams*, pp. 126-127, Third Edition, Digireads.com Publishing, 2010
2 S. Freud, *The Interpretation of Dreams*, p. 278, Third Edition, Digireads.com Publishing, 2010
3 S. Freud, *Moses And Monotheism*, pp. 32-33, First American Edition, 1939
4 H.P. Lovecraft, *The Complete Fiction*, "The Colour Out of Space," pp.614-615, Barnes and Nobles, Inc., 2008
5 *Encyclopaedia Britannica*, 11th edition, Volume 10, New York, The Encyclopaedia Britannica Company, 1910
6 Lewis Carrol, *Alice's Adventures in Wonderland*, pp. 184-185, BookVirtual Corp, 2000
7 N. Land, *Fanged Noumena*, pp. 447-448, Urbanomic, 2018
8 J.P. Sartre, *Existentialism Is A* 52-53, Yale University Press, 2007
9 N. Land, *Fanged Noumena*, 454, Urbanomic 2018
10 J.P. Sartre, *Existentialism Is A Humanism*, pp. 52-53, Yale University Press, 2007
11 N. Land, *Fanged Noumena*, 454, Urbanomic 2018
12 M.L. King, "I Have A Dream," Spoken, August 28, 1963
13 N. Machiavelli, *Discourses on Levy*, p. 119, Oxford University Press, 2003
14 S. Zizek, verbally, repeatedly, 2010-
15 G.W.F Hegel, *Philosophy of Right*, p. 109, Oxford University Press, 2008
16 G.W.F Hegel, *Philosophy of Right*, p. 228, Oxford University Press, 2008
17 M. Stirner, *Ego and his Own*, p. 3, Dover Books, 2005
18 G.W.F Hegel, *Philosophy of Right*, p. 228, Oxford University Press, 2008

CULTURE, SOCIETY & POLITICS

The modern world is at an impasse. Disasters scroll across our
smartphone screens and we're invited to like, follow or upvote,
but critical thinking is harder and harder to find. Rather than
connecting us in common struggle and debate, the internet has
sped up and deepened a long-standing process of alienation and
atomization. Zer0 Books wants to work against this trend.
With critical theory as our jumping off point, we aim to publish
books that make our readers uncomfortable. We want to move
beyond received opinions.
Zer0 Books is on the left and wants to reinvent the left. We are
sick of the injustice, the suffering and the stupidity that defines
both our political and cultural world, and we aim to find a new
foundation for a new struggle.

If this book has helped you to clarify an idea, solve a problem or
extend your knowledge, you may want to check out our online
content as well. Look for Zer0 Books: Advancing Conversations
in the iTunes directory and for our Zer0 Books YouTube channel.

Popular videos include:

Žižek and the Double Blackmain

The Intellectual Dark Web is a Bad Sign

Can there be an Anti-SJW Left?

Answering Jordan Peterson on Marxism

Follow us on Facebook
at https://www.facebook.com/ZeroBooks and Twitter at https://
twitter.com/Zer0Books

Bestsellers from Zer0 Books include:

Give Them An Argument
Logic for the Left
Ben Burgis
Many serious leftists have learned to distrust talk of logic. This is
a serious mistake.
Paperback: 978-1-78904-210-8 ebook: 978-1-78904-211-5

Poor but Sexy
Culture Clashes in Europe East and West
Agata Pyzik
How the East stayed East and the West stayed West.
Paperback: 978-1-78099-394-2 ebook: 978-1-78099-395-9

An Anthropology of Nothing in Particular
Martin Demant Frederiksen
A journey into the social lives of meaninglessness.
Paperback: 978-1-78535-699-5 ebook: 978-1-78535-700-8

Cartographies of the Absolute
Alberto Toscano, Jeff Kinkle
An aesthetics of the economy for the twenty-first century.
Paperback: 978-1-78099-275-4 ebook: 978-1-78279-973-3

Malign Velocities
Accelerationism and Capitalism
Benjamin Noys
Long listed for the Bread and Roses Prize 2015, *Malign Velocities*
argues against the need for speed, tracking acceleration
as the symptom of the ongoing crises of capitalism.
Paperback: 978-1-78279-300-7 ebook: 978-1-78279-299-4

Meat Market
Female Flesh under Capitalism
Laurie Penny
A feminist dissection of women's bodies as the fleshy fulcrum of
capitalist cannibalism, whereby women are both consumers and
consumed.
Paperback: 978-1-84694-521-2 ebook: 978-1-84694-782-7

Babbling Corpse
Vaporwave and the Commodification of Ghosts
Grafton Tanner
Paperback: 978-1-78279-759-3 ebook: 978-1-78279-760-9

New Work New Culture
Work we want and a culture that strengthens us
Frithjoff Bergmann
A serious alternative for mankind and the planet.
Paperback: 978-1-78904-064-7 ebook: 978-1-78904-065-4

Romeo and Juliet in Palestine
Teaching Under Occupation
Tom Sperlinger
Life in the West Bank, the nature of pedagogy and the role of a
university under occupation.
Paperback: 978-1-78279-637-4 ebook: 978-1-78279-636-7

Ghosts of My Life
Writings on Depression, Hauntology and Lost Futures
Mark Fisher
Paperback: 978-1-78099-226-6 ebook: 978-1-78279-624-4

Sweetening the Pill
or How We Got Hooked on Hormonal Birth Control
Holly Grigg-Spall
Has contraception liberated or oppressed women?
Sweetening the Pill breaks the silence on the dark side of hormonal
contraception.
Paperback: 978-1-78099-607-3 ebook: 978-1-78099-608-0

Why Are We The Good Guys?
Reclaiming Your Mind from the Delusions of Propaganda
David Cromwell
A provocative challenge to the standard ideology that Western
power is a benevolent force in the world.
Paperback: 978-1-78099-365-2 ebook: 978-1-78099-366-9

The Writing on the Wall
On the Decomposition of Capitalism and its Critics
Anselm Jappe, Alastair Hemmens
A new approach to the meaning of social emancipation.
Paperback: 978-1-78535-581-3 ebook: 978-1-78535-582-0

Enjoying It
Candy Crush and Capitalism
Alfie Bown
A study of enjoyment and of the enjoyment of studying. Bown
asks what enjoyment says about us and what we say about
enjoyment, and why.
Paperback: 978-1-78535-155-6 ebook: 978-1-78535-156-3

Color, Facture, Art and Design
Iona Singh
This materialist definition of fine-art develops guidelines for
architecture, design, cultural-studies and ultimately social
change.
Paperback: 978-1-78099-629-5 ebook: 978-1-78099-630-1

Neglected or Misunderstood
The Radical Feminism of Shulamith Firestone
Victoria Margree
An interrogation of issues surrounding gender, biology,
sexuality, work and technology, and the ways in which our
imaginations continue to be in thrall to ideologies of maternity
and the nuclear family.
Paperback: 978-1-78535-539-4 ebook: 978-1-78535-540-0

How to Dismantle the NHS in 10 Easy Steps (Second Edition)
Youssef El-Gingihy
The story of how your NHS was sold off and why you will have
to buy private health insurance soon. A new expanded second
edition with chapters on junior doctors' strikes and government
blueprints for US-style healthcare.
Paperback: 978-1-78904-178-1 ebook: 978-1-78904-179-8

Digesting Recipes
The Art of Culinary Notation
Susannah Worth
A recipe is an instruction, the imperative tone of the expert, but this constraint can offer its own kind of potential. A recipe need not be a domestic trap but might instead offer escape – something to fantasise about or aspire to.
Paperback: 978-1-78279-860-6 ebook: 978-1-78279-859-0

Most titles are published in paperback and as an ebook. Paperbacks are available in traditional bookshops. Both print and ebook formats are available online.
Follow us on Facebook
at https://www.facebook.com/ZeroBooks
and Twitter at https://twitter.com/Zer0Books